AND
I SHALL
DWELL
AMONG THEM

MAKE FOR ME A SANCTUARY,

AND I SHALL DWELL AMONG THEM. . . .

—EXODUS 25:8

AND I SHALL DWELL AMONG THEM

HISTORIC SYNAGOGUES OF THE WORLD

PHOTOGRAPHS BY
NEIL FOLBERG

ESSAY BY
YOM TOV ASSIS

AN APERTURE BOOK

CONTENTS

THE CROWN OF THE ELDERLY IS THEIR GRANDCHILDREN.
FATHERS ARE A CROWN FOR THEIR SONS, AND THE SONS ARE A CROWN FOR THEIR FATHERS.
—BREISHIT RABBA, TOLDOT

FOR MY PARENTS AND MY CHILDREN
N. F.

בס״ד

THIS PUBLICATION IS SUPPORTED BY GENEROUS CONTRIBUTIONS FROM:

MARJORIE AND IRVING COWAN, LEONARD FRIEDLAND, AND ANNETTE AND JACK FRIEDLAND,
IN LOVING MEMORY OF SAMUEL NATHAN FRIEDLAND.

STEVEN AMES AND THE HARRIETT AMES CHARITABLE TRUST,
IN LOVING MEMORY OF HARRIETT AMES.

JOSEPH FOLBERG PROVIDED ESSENTIAL SUPPORT FOR THE EXTENSIVE TRAVEL
AND THE PUBLICATION OF THE BOOK. HIS GUIDANCE AND UNWAVERING GOOD WILL HAVE BEEN AND
CONTINUE TO BE MEANINGFUL TO ALL CONCERNED IN THE FULFILLMENT OF THIS WORK.

ADDITIONAL SUPPORT FOR THE PHOTOGRAPHIC WORK WAS PROVIDED BY:
THE BY-PROD CORPORATION, DAVID DEVINE, EL-AL ISRAEL AIRLINES,
MICHAEL ELIAS, ERIC E. ESTORICK, GEORGEANNE AND JAMES GARFINKEL,
THE DAVID H. GLUCK FOUNDATION, THE RICHARD AND RHODA GOLDMAN FUND,
ARTHUR GOODWIN, HADAR PHOTO AGENCIES, F. ROD HOLT,
WALTER AND JOSEPHINE LANDOR, THE JOE AND EMILY LOWE FOUNDATION,
RICHARD SMOOKE, AND VISION GALLERY, SAN FRANCISCO.

APERTURE FOUNDATION IS DEEPLY GRATEFUL TO THESE SUPPORTERS AND
TO ALL THOSE WHO ASSISTED THE PHOTOGRAPHER, NEIL FOLBERG, IN HIS TRAVELS TO
ENSURE THE COMPLETION OF THIS UNPRECEDENTED PROJECT.

A PLACE OF GATHERING,
A PLACE OF LIGHT
NEIL FOLBERG

Make for Me a Sanctuary, and I shall dwell among them. . . .
—Exodus 25:8

When Israel gathers to pray, they do not pray together as one, but each and every synagogue prays by itself: first this synagogue and then the next one. And when all the congregations have finished all their prayers, the angel responsible for prayer takes all the prayers from all the synagogues and makes of them crowns to place upon the head of the Holy One, Blessed be He. . . .
—Midrash Shmot Rabba, Seder Beshalach

From the ends of the earth I have gathered together a visual memento of Jewish communities to bring them together in this book—a crown, if you will, for the Jewish people. But only an angel could actually finish this task, for Jews are found in virtually every country and have been nearly everywhere at one time or another. My approach has been subjective and selective: to evoke something of the spirit and cultural environment of each community, while showing the diversity of architecture and ornamentation, reflecting the spiritual aspirations, esthetics, and story of the people who built the synagogues, and in many cases continue to use them.

A hundred years ago, this project would have required the dedicated lifetime of an intrepid adventurer, given the difficulties of travel and the dispersion of Jews to places where only the slightest trace of their existence remains. Travel today is of course easier, but many places are now in ruins, or no longer exist at all; numerous synagogues have been converted to warehouses and cultural centers, libraries, mosques, and churches. Their original form and function have been lost in layers of dust and paint, so that now only an aficionado can find in them something of interest.

Even so, there were too many places for anyone to visit, so I chose among the older synagogues that are still in good condition. Many of these synagogues have been well documented; others will be unknown even to experts. Each of my readers will be able to tell me about a synagogue I should have photographed, one that is close to the heart. But I hope that, looking through these pages, you will find another that evokes the spirit of the place you know.

Seen in this light, the photographs in this book are personal documents. I often came to pray in these buildings a few moments alone, before the others arrived, or remained for a while after they left. In synagogues that are no longer used or are used infrequently, I could only imagine the presence of the congregation. If someone entered your home in your absence, he could study the pictures on the wall, browse among the objects on the desk, and look through the books to know something about you. In this way, I tried to make a photograph of an empty room that nevertheless portrays the existence of the people who use it and the minds that planned it. I hope to have revealed some aspect of the collective personality of the congregation, and

I trust my image will say, "This is my place, the chair where I sit while I watch the play of light during the first hours of the day on the Sabbath morning."

This brings me to discuss a process that I hope will remain largely hidden to my viewers, not because it is a secret but because it is only a means to an end. That means is photographic technique and the end product is an esthetic statement, the photograph. The art critic Jacob Bronowski says that when we look at an artist's work, we must ask the question, "Why did the artist make it this way?" A very brief discussion of my technique may allow you some insight.

The first material form that God created was light. With this light, He began to bring order into the universe. Using light, He defined the central nature of the universe. Just so, the artist uses light to create mood and define the objects in his small universe. Working in the confined space of a room, however large, gave me the opportunity at least to help shape the light, if not to create light that suited my purpose.

Here was a level of creativity that previously had not been available to me, but of course each measure of freedom brings with it its own restrictions. I brought to these synagogues my own lighting equipment and a talented assistant, Max Richardson, who had much valuable experience in lighting. We carried about one hundred kilos of gear, consisting of two cases of electronic flash equipment and another bag of stands, tripods, extension cords, and a multitude of strange plug adapters that we came to call by the names of the countries they came from: "Uzbekistan," "Morocco," "Germany," and so forth. In order to light spaces as large as those we were working in, with a sum total of seven flash units, we had to use a combination of available and flash light.

Sometimes the flash was the main light we had to use to override the existing light, but often we used it to spot certain areas or to fill in the dark shadows. Only in rare cases did I make a photograph with just one exposure, however long, that was suitable for both the flash and the existing light. Rather, I devised a working technique that allowed us to separate the ambient exposure completely from the many flash exposures.

These photographs, then, were formed by a multitude of exposures layered upon one another on a single sheet of film—sometimes as many as fifty exposures for a single image. This made it impossible to include any object that was not absolutely stable. Chandeliers blowing in the wind had to be tied as best we could to prevent movement or you would have seen not one blurry image, but many sharp ghost-images. And of course, this also prevented us from including people in any of the photos made with multiple exposures. This technique, though, had the advantage of allowing me to photograph an image that existed only in my mind.

Had you walked in on us while we were making a photograph, you might have tripped over a cord in the darkness. You certainly would not have seen the synagogue as it looks in these photographs. How then, you might ask, does it really look? It looks a little bit like the photograph, depending on what time of day or night you visit it, how much you know of its people,

VIEW FROM
THE ARON KODESH,
FLORENCE, ITALY

customs, prayers, and history—and what you had for breakfast. In short, it looks the way you see it. These photographs, then, show the way I saw it.

Some thoughts on the architecture of the synagogue: In a cathedral, it seems to me, one is made to feel small before the glory of God. The emphasis in a grand church is placed on the divine aspect of the man-God relationship. God is great and beautiful, while we are small and insignificant, and the architecture becomes a spatial metaphor for that principle. Jews, by contrast, are responsible for bringing sanctity into their own lives and do not expect it as a gift from above, as some kind of divine grace.

There is an allegorical story that tells of how we may prepare ourselves for the Divine Presence. A king wishes to have dinner at the home of his close friend. This man has only simple furnishings, with which he prepares for his royal guest. But as the king, grandly decked with servants and gold lamps, approaches his friend's humble home, the friend is ashamed of his ordinary furnishings and quickly puts everything away.

When the king came to his door . . . he asked, "Why haven't you prepared anything?" The friend explained that he had seen the king coming with his royal entourage and became embarrassed, so he had put everything away. The king exclaimed, "I will send away all that I have brought with me and use only your things." So Israel made the Sanctuary, placing the menorah in it. Only when they had made all ready did the Divine Presence enter.

—Bamindbar Rabba, Seder Baha'alotchah

In Hebrew we call the synagogue *beth knesset*—a place of gathering—which emphasizes not the nature of its use, but the community that uses it. In a traditional Orthodox *beth knesset*, there are two poles of activity, one in the center of the building, among the people: that is the *bimah*, where the Torah is read. The other is in front of the people, representing divinity: that is the *aron kodesh*, where the Torah scroll is kept. The architectural emphasis may be oriented to the front, though in several of these synagogues the focus is in the center. During the service, though, we remove the Torah scroll and place it among us in the central space. Here is where all the action takes place. It is the interaction between the *bimah* and the *aron kodesh* that symbolizes human interaction with the divine.

Once the Divine Presence entered the Shaf V'Yetev Synagogue in Babylon, terrifying Rav Sheshet. He pleaded, "Lord of the Universe, I am a lowly creature, but must I yield to the Heavenly Host, or they to me?" God commanded the Heavenly Host, "Let him be!"

—Talmud Bavli, Tractate Megilah

The synagogue, the *beth knesset*, is not a place where we receive a sacrament from a priest at the altar. It is a place where we try to create holiness among ourselves that we can take into our lives. We build the altar within ourselves by dedicating our actions to God. These are the commandments that apply to every aspect of our daily lives.

*At the time when the Holy One, Blessed be He, said to Moses, "Make for Me a Sanctuary. . . ,"
Moses wondered: "The glory of the Holy One, Blessed be He, fills the Heavens and the Earth.
How, then, can He command me, 'Make for Me a Sanctuary. . .'?"*

—Midrash Shmot Rabba, Seder Terumah

*. . .The rationale behind the Sanctuary is not the materials from which it was made. The essential
lesson of the Sanctuary is that we should purify our hearts, in order to allow the Divine Presence
to rest in us. . . .*

—Me'am Lo'ez, Shmot Terumah

We are taught that humankind is at the center of the universe, just as the *bimah* is at the center of the synagogue. Rabbi Schneur Zalman, the great Hasidic rabbi who founded the Lubavitch dynasty in Russia, wrote in *Sefer Hatanya* that

*the ultimate purpose of Creation is this lowest world, for such was His blessed will that He shall
have satisfaction when . . . the darkness is turned into light.*

—Likutei Amarim

Since we were made "in the image of God," we are imbued with Godlike attributes. We can participate in creation by turning darkness into light, by illuminating the darkness with the light of truth. Light naturally overpowers darkness: think of a single candle in a dark cavern. This is the function of those who serve God; it is also the purpose of the artist, who may use light not only to define his subject, but also to reveal its deeper significance.

THE MEDITERRANEAN
ITALY, MOROCCO, AND TURKEY

Windows are usually made narrow on the outside and wider inside, so that the light coming from outside will spread in the interior, but in the Beit Hamikdash we were commanded to do the opposite. The windows there were made wider on the outside and narrower inside to show that the light from the Beit Hamikdash lights the world. . . .
—Me'am Loez, Shmot Tezaveh

The pagan temples, churches, and mosques of the Mediterranean lands stand boldly on sunny hill-tops, while the synagogues are more often found in the lanes of the marketplace, in a courtyard, or on

ALESSANDRIA, ITALY (left)
CEILING, ALESSANDRIA, ITALY (above)

the top floor of a ghetto dwelling. The sacred monuments of the Gentiles are lit by the sun; the Jewish edifices must provide their own light from within, like a home.

The small town of Mondovi, in the Piemonte district of Italy, sits on a hill amidst fields. At the very top of the hill is the bell tower of the church. Nearby, nestled in a tight cluster of buildings, is the single apartment house that was the Jewish ghetto. At one time, all the Jewish families of the town lived in this one building, whose uppermost floor was dedicated to the synagogue. The Jews have all gone, save one Mr. Levi; the synagogue remains under his care and that of its Gentile neighbors. When I visited one afternoon, Mr. Levi had lit all the candles in the building, since electric lights had never been installed. The soft light enveloped us as we entered, making this interior space seem bright. A group of us prayed the afternoon service together—the first time in decades that a prayer service had been conducted there.

The Italian, Turkish, and Moroccan synagogues have little in common with one another besides a modest manner of presenting themselves to the world. In Mondovi, you have to knock on the ground-floor tenant's door to get the key, then climb stairs until you arrive at the entrance to the synagogue—which looks little different from the other doors in the house.

In Izmir, Turkey, the synagogues were in the narrow lanes of the market and could only be reached on foot, so that I had to hire a porter to cart my equipment. Once there, I would find myself in front of a simple door. I would sit down on the lighting cases while I waited for my guide to locate the person with the key. Through the door is a courtyard; inside the courtyard, there is often yet another door leading into the synagogue. The experience is like passing through a series of locks on a canal.

In Tangier, Morocco, there are several synagogues on Rue des Synagogues in the *mellah*—the Jewish part of the old town. In this anonymous street, with its closed doors and small cluttered antique

Lag B'omer at grave of Rabbi Ihya, Morocco (above)

Afternoon prayers at the Signora Synagogue, Izmir, Turkey (above left)

Entrance to a synagogue in the marketplace, Izmir, Turkey (above)

Entrance to the ghetto (left), the ghetto (above), Venice, Italy

shop, is an imposing residence that once belonged to Moshe Nahon, one of the leading members of the Jewish community. Nearby is the Nahon synagogue, which has just been restored. I'd been told that the synagogue possessed a lovely collection of silver lamps, but when we entered, we found the place in a shambles, and wires hanging where the lamps had been. I located the lamps in the Jewish community office, where they were being polished. It took some persuasion, but eventually we received permission to hang five of the larger lamps ourselves. I found myself supervising a crew, consisting of a man from the Jewish home for the aged, the Muslim caretaker, my assistant Max, and our driver. On our first day of work in this space, we mopped the floor, dusted the furniture, and hung lamps. We tried the lamps here and there, until they looked just right.

This synagogue actually seemed rather grand once the lamps were hung. They gleamed brilliantly against the dark wooden *aron kodesh* and muted tones of the stucco interior. Max polished the stone floor and I made a photograph. When I came back to show the synagogue to a visitor the next Shabbat, I noticed that three more lamps had been hung.

The numerous lamps are a unique feature of the Moroccan synagogues. The *Me'am Loez* states that, just as it was once praiseworthy to donate oil for the eternal lamp in the Temple, so it is a good deed to donate oil for the lamps in a synagogue, bringing blessings upon the donor and his family.

Rebbe Hayyim Ben Attar is a perfect example of the learned and worldly Mediterranean Jew. Born in Morocco in 1696, he set out for the Holy Land by way of Italy, where he stayed for two years, residing in Livorno and Venice, before departing for Jerusalem. Once there, he established two rabbinical seminaries, or *yeshivot*. He died at the age of forty-seven, and is buried on the Mount of Olives, where these words are engraved on his tombstone: "The Land of Israel was enlightened by his glory, as from the illumination of the seven-branched menorah."

In a commentary he wrote on the Torah, called the *Or Hayyim* (Light of life), Ben Attar discusses the oil used to light the menorah in the Temple: "Pure olive oil represents the Torah that is compared to oil, for just as oil provides light for the world, so does Torah."

Dar Al-Mae Synagogue (now a private Muslim home), Fez, Morocco (below)

Haliwah family, Marrakech, Morocco (right)

Home of Moshe Haliwah, Marrakech, Morocco (right, above)

Entrance to Ibn-Danan Synagogue (door at left), Fez, Morocco (top)

Hananya El-Fasi (Berber Jews) at the tomb of R. Ben Lanhash, Morocco (above)

ARON KODESH,
CANTON SYNAGOGUE,
VENICE, ITALY (top)

ENTRANCE,
CANTON SYNAGOGUE,
VENICE, ITALY (bottom)

ITALY

CANTON SYNAGOGUE,
VENICE, ITALY

FLORENCE, ITALY

ARON KODESH,
TEDESCA SYNAGOGUE,
VENICE, ITALY (opposite)

ARON KODESH
AND BIMAH,
FLORENCE, ITALY

MONDOVI, ITALY (above)

ARCHES, FLORENCE,
ITALY (opposite)

SALUZZO, ITALY

ARON KODESH
WITH TORAH SCROLLS,
BIELLA, ITALY (opposite)

CASALE MONFERRATO,
ITALY

MOROCCO

NAHON SYNAGOGUE,
TANGIER, MOROCCO

WINDOWS,
NAHON SYNAGOGUE,
TANGIER, MOROCCO
(OPPOSITE)

SUIRI SYNAGOGUE,
TANGIER, MOROCCO

ARON KODESH,
SADOUN SYNAGOGUE,
FEZ, MOROCCO

ARON KODESH,
SUIRI SYNAGOGUE,
TANGIER, MOROCCO
(opposite)

*LAMPS,
CASABLANCA,
MOROCCO (top)*

*ARON KODESH,
IBN-DANAN SYNAGOGUE,
FEZ, MOROCCO (bottom)*

*SEFER TORAH,
SADOUN SYNAGOGUE,
FEZ, MOROCCO
(opposite)*

TURKEY

TORAH SCROLLS,
SIGNORA SYNAGOGUE,
IZMIR, TURKEY

SIGNORA SYNAGOGUE,
IZMIR, TURKEY
(opposite)

BIMAH,
BIKUR HOLIM SYNAGOGUE,
IZMIR, TURKEY

BIKUR HOLIM SYNAGOGUE,
IZMIR, TURKEY

YAMBOLI SYNAGOGUE,
ISTANBUL, TURKEY
(overleaf)

ASIA
UZBEKISTAN AND INDIA

It came to pass in the days of Ahashverosh, this is the Ahashverosh who rules over one-hundred and twenty-seven countries from India to Ethiopia. . . .

So begins the Book of Esther, the scroll that Jews read on the festival of Purim. This book tells the story of the Jews of Persia, who were saved from destruction at the hands of their enemies in the land to which they were exiled after Jerusalem was razed. From the ancient kingdom of Ahashverosh, whose capital was in modern Iran, the Jews spread throughout Asia: to Bukhara (Uzbekistan)—where the Jews still speak a dialect closely related to Persian—and even to India, where I heard the reader in a Bombay synagogue reciting the words above from a handwritten parchment scroll.

After the Babylonian conquest of Israel in the sixth century B.C.E., Jews dispersed throughout

EZRAT NASHIM, KALANTAROV HOUSE, SAMARKAND, UZBEKISTAN (left)

KALANTAROV HOUSE SYNAGOGUE, SAMARKAND, UZBEKISTAN (above)

Mesopotamia and from there to Persia and Central Asia. The members of the Bene Israel community in northern India say of themselves that they date back to the second century B.C.E. I held in my hands the 1,000-year-old copper plates granting land and privilege to the Jews of Cochin, India, for "as long as the world and moon exist."

The Jews of Cochin, like the Chinese in San Francisco, live in a part of town that is distinctly theirs: Jew Town. There used to be three synagogues in Cochin, but today the community has dwindled to twenty-two souls, and only the Pardesi synagogue remains in use. (Another one has been packed and shipped to Israel, where it has been installed in the Israel Museum.) The Jews themselves have left for more active centers of Jewish life. This community has not seen persecution at the hands of the native Indians, who seem to consider the Jews an integral and accepted part of the land. Only during periods of European rule have the Jews of India suffered, for most of the Christian colonial powers brought their prejudices with them.

There are other synagogues in the Cochin district, in nearby Ernakulam, Parur, and Chennamangalam. The latter is a village set amid towering palm trees in an area rich with brilliant green rice paddies and flowing water. There, in the midst of this lush jungle, is a deserted synagogue that stands beside a well, abandoned. Unfortunately, no one has keys, and we were unable to enter.

We had more luck when we visited one of the few Jewish families in Parur. From their house we went to the synagogue, a structure unlike any I have seen. From the street entrance, you pass through simple wooden doors that lead into a small courtyard. Beyond the palms is another passageway that leads to a covered colonnade and another door. Here you find yourself in the middle of a spacious lot, now overgrown with weeds; once, it must have been a lovely garden. Through the next door is an entrance hall, and beyond that the synagogue itself, with a massive wooden *aron* and the *bimah* in the center of the room. Our hosts told us that the synagogue is still in use, but its appearance belied their words: it looked as if no one had used it for years.

In ten years' time, there will no longer be a Jewish community in Cochin. The Jews there are philosophical about the process, for they are not fleeing persecution as so many others have, but are leaving for life in a Jewish state. They will leave the Pardesi synagogue behind—it will probably become a museum supported by the state. They will also be leaving behind traditions that will never be successfully transplanted elsewhere, no matter how tight the community remains, and no matter how hard they try to preserve them.

The modest Bene Israel synagogues in the region of Bombay date only to the last century, but have

Men studying, Bene Israel Synagogue, Bombay, India

Sha'are Ratson Synagogue, Bombay, India (above)

Courtyard entrance of synagogue, Parur, India (right, above)

Abandoned synagogue, Chennamangalam, India (right)

Prayer in Magen Avot Synagogue, Alibag, India

both color and charm. When I first saw them, they seemed less than impressive; but when I looked at the photographs upon returning to Israel, I knew I had a treasure, for the synagogues share a straightforward unpretentiousness with the people who pray in them.

One day we made a gruelling drive from Bombay to Alibag, perhaps three hours through congestion and pollution to cover a distance of not more than fifty kilometers. We got there just as it was getting dark, and we dashed over to the synagogue in order to see it before night fell. There we found an island of purity, a simple, colorful building set among the palms in a walled-off yard. It fit in with its surroundings, but it was distinct nevertheless. The Passover Haggadah tells of the Jews in ancient Egypt: "They became there a nation, which teaches us that Israel retained their distinctive qualities. . . ." The *Shivlei Leket* explains this passage, saying: "Even though they were few in number they were not swallowed among the multitudes of Egypt, but rather they maintained their distinctiveness in religion and customs. They were known and recognized as a nation unto themselves." There is no better description of the Bene Israel in India, whose very name indicates an allegience to their people and faith, for "Bene Israel" means "Children of Israel."

There was a sense of urgency in our trip to Uzbekistan. The Center for Jewish Art at the Hebrew University in Jerusalem had indicated that it was important that I go, since Jews were steadily leaving the area. It was not a flight of panic, but every day that passed meant that there might be one more place that would be sold to non-Jews or become inaccessible for lack of a key.

As we flew over Uzbekistan, I watched the steppes below in trepidation—there was not a single sign of life to be seen: no roads, homes, streets, not even trees. We landed in Tashkent and walked down the stairs from the plane in absolute blackness. On the plane, an Israeli who had been there before had asked me: "How long are you staying?" I said, "We're staying three weeks. We're here to photograph synagogues for a book." "Three weeks?" he said. "I'll tell you what: you'll stay until your toilet paper runs out, then you'll leave like everybody else." I laughed at the Israeli (I could afford to laugh: we had ample supplies of toilet paper with us), but as we kicked up layers of dust upon entering the terminal I wondered if my laughter hadn't been premature.

We were met by Rafi Nektalov and his wife Miriam, who were to help us for the following weeks. That has been my chief comfort throughout this project: wherever we have gone we have found people we could trust and with whom we shared common bonds, no matter how different our cultures were or how far apart we were on religious issues. It often made me feel that I had traveled all that way only to arrive where I had begun, in the Jewish world.

We arrived shivering and exhausted in Samarkand in the early morning darkness and made our way through the unlit streets to the *makhla*, the Jewish quarter. As we passed through the streets, we were greeted with a *shalom* from everyone and an occasional Hebrew phrase. These people have survived decades of Communist suppression of religion and Jewish education. Though they are largely unaware of Jewish tradition, there are a few things the Bukharan Jews have managed to hang on to: a minimal observance of *kashrut*, the Jewish dietary laws, and a very strong Jewish identity.

Blossom Esther Hallegua with her Shabbat table, Cochin, India (above)

Wedding preparations, Bombay, India (right, top and bottom)

CEILING DETAIL,
KALANTAROV HOUSE SYNAGOGUE,
SAMARKAND, UZBEKISTAN

UZBEKISTAN

KALANTAROV HOUSE
SYNAGOGUE,
SAMARKAND, UZBEKISTAN

נשלם זה הבנין זשנ ת
תרס ליצירה
רחתמו

RUBINOV HOUSE
SYNAGOGUE,
BUKHARA,
UZBEKISTAN

*SHARBATI FAMILY
SYNAGOGUE, BUKHARA,
UZBEKISTAN (top)*

*ZEVULONOV
HOUSE SYNAGOGUE,
SAMARKAND,
UZBEKISTAN (bottom)*

ZEVULONOV HOUSE
SYNAGOGUE,
SAMARKAND, UZBEKISTAN

CARVED WOODEN BIMAH,
GUMBAS SYNAGOGUE,
SAMARKAND, UZBEKISTAN

STUDY OF WINDOW,
GUMBAS SYNAGOGUE,
SAMARKAND,
UZBEKISTAN (opposite)

INDIA

LEN HALLEGUA,
PARDESI SYNAGOGUE,
COCHIN, INDIA

SHA'ARE RATSON
SYNAGOGUE, BOMBAY,
INDIA (opposite)

MAGEN AVOT
SYNAGOGUE, ALIBAG,
INDIA (above)

ELIJAH'S CHAIRS,
BEIT-EL SYNAGOGUE,
PANVEL, INDIA
(above)

ARON KODESH,
SHAAREI RAHAMIM
SYNAGOGUE, BOMBAY,
INDIA *(opposite)*

MAGEN DAVID SYNAGOGUE, BOMBAY, INDIA

NORTH SIDE OF
SYNAGOGUE,
PARUR, INDIA (top)

COVERED WALKWAY,
PARUR, INDIA (bottom)

PORCH,
BEIT-EL SYNAGOGUE,
RAUDENDA, INDIA

THE AMERICAS
THE CARIBBEAN,
THE UNITED STATES, AND CANADA

Happily the government of the United States, which gives to bigotry no sanction, to persecution no assistance, requires only that they who live under its protection should demean themselves as good citizens. . . . May the Children of Abraham, who dwell in this land, continue to merit and enjoy the good will of the other Inhabitants; while every one shall sit in safety under his own vine and fig tree and there shall be none to make him afraid.
   —letter from George Washington to the
      Hebrew Congregation in Newport, R.I., 1790

KINGSTON, JAMAICA, WEST INDIES (left)

TOMBSTONES, SHAAR HASHAMAYIM SYNAGOGUE, KINGSTON, JAMAICA, WEST INDIES (above)

That was the promise made by America's first president to the Jews of the United States, a promise that has been kept through many generations. There has been no safer haven for the Jews than the Americas, but it is a story that goes back further than the founding of the American colonies—perhaps as far back as the discovery of the American continent by the Europeans. It is quite possible that Christopher Columbus was a *converso*, a Jew practicing his religion in secret after having been converted by either force or force of circumstance by the Spanish monarchs Ferdinand and Isabella. The Jews of Spain were exiled in 1492, the same year that Columbus sailed from the country they had come to regard as their own. It would be over a hundred years before significant numbers of Jews found refuge in the New World, settling first in the West Indies, the islands of the Caribbean, and on the northern shores of South America.

In the early seventeenth century, Jews settled on the island of Barbados; they came to Curaçao with the Dutch in the 1650s and by 1655 they had formed a community in Jamaica at Port Royal. The buildings that I visited on these islands were built much later than that, as the original synagogues had been damaged by hurricanes or torn down.

I encountered this chapter of Jewish history as I wandered through the cemetery that adjoins the Nidhe Yisrael Synagogue in Barbados. Tombstones can be found here that date back to the seventeenth century. The epitaphs are terse, but the motifs depicted include the skull and crossbones, or a hand reaching from the heavens to chop down a young tree. I wandered among the dead for a while before entering the synagogue, which is now active and restored to its original condition after a period of neglect.

Today, the Jews in Barbados cannot trace their ancestry back very far, as the descendants of the original settlers have long since gone and been replaced by others. But it is a different story in Curaçao and Jamaica, where many can follow the genealogy of their families back for generations.

The Mikveh Israel synagogue in Willemstad, Curaçao, was modeled after the most famous Spanish and Portuguese synagogue in Amsterdam; however, at least superficially, it bears little resemblance to its model. As in Amsterdam, there are two large columns at the entrance, named "Yachin" and "Boaz "(after the pillars of the Temple in Jerusalem) and the *tevah*, or reading stand, is found at the extreme western wall near the entrance. Here the resemblance ends. While the synagogue in Amsterdam is a stone building, Mikveh Israel is stucco, painted a rich yellow. From the interior, you look at bright sun-painted plaster through windows capped with deep-blue glass. The courtyard of the synagogue, broad and bright, leads into the street through a gate adorned with the inscription, "May you be blessed upon leaving," and should you turn around, you will see the words "May you be blessed upon entering" in Hebrew above the gate. The floor of Mikveh Israel is covered with sand, as it is in the Shaar Hashamayim synagogue in Kingston, Jamaica, and as it once was in Barbados and Amsterdam. The sand is another of the unique customs of the Spanish *conversos*, who, it is said, spread sand on the floor of their meeting places so that the Inquisition would not hear the footsteps of the clandestine worshipers. Or perhaps it is a remembrance of the sand of Sinai through which the People of Israel had to pass in their flight to freedom.

In any event, the *conversos* remained wary of the long arm of the Inquisition for centuries. In the United States, the secret trapdoor in the floor of the *bimah* of the Touro synagogue in Newport, Rhode Island, demonstrates their unease. In the late 1700s a Dutch Jew by the name of Isaac Touro settled in Jamaica; his son was among the supporters of the Touro synagogue in Rhode Island, which was designed by Peter Harrison, an English sea captain from York. Construction on the building began in 1759.

According to legend, when the British forces captured Newport from the rebellious colonists they burned all but two of its public buildings. The Anglican Church (loyal to the Crown) was of course spared. When the British soldiers entered the synagogue, their commander told them to spare also this building from the torch. Rabbi Shapiro, who now presides at Touro, thinks that the commander may have misunderstood the meaning of the three crowns painted above the *aron kodesh*. The crowns symbolize the three crowns given to the Jewish people: the crown of Torah, of Kingdom, and of the Priesthood—but they may well have been taken as Royalist

Four generations of Maduro family, Willemstad, Curaçao, West Indies (top)

Tomb of a merchant, Kingston, Jamaica, West Indies (above)

emblems. So, as one of the few public buildings to survive the Revolution, the Touro synagogue stood and served the Rhode Island legislature as well as the Supreme Court for many years.

The Touro synagogue is truly magnificent, and among the most famous in the world, but in general I've found that I am drawn to the more humble and lesser-known synagogues. It was this inclination that led me to explore some of the small towns of the southern states. Starting from New Orleans, I drove along the Mississippi River to Natchez, Port Gibson, and Brookhaven, visiting synagogues. Jews had come to live in these towns as farmers and merchants. In recent years, the Jewish populations have dwindled here, as people migrated to large urban centers; nevertheless, nearly all the congregations I visited are still active.

In Brookhaven, I found a plain white wooden synagogue that looked for all the world like a Baptist church, so completely had the Jews borrowed from local architectural idioms. The local *Daily Leader* proudly advertises this edifice: "One stop on Brookhaven's Tour of Homes has its roots in a tradition that goes not only back to the early days of Brookhaven, but back to the early days of history. . . ." It is known locally as "the oldest active Jewish congregation in Mississippi."

The prize of Mississippi synagogue architecture is the flamboyant structure in Port Gibson, which

boasts towers and an onion dome, and which is described in the Mississippi Department of Archives and History as "Victorian Moro-Byzantine Revival." It is located next to a filling station on the main street of Port Gibson—the town General Grant declared "too beautiful to burn." In Port Gibson, I stayed at the restored bed-and-breakfast of Henry and Martha Lumm, the couple that bought the synagogue from Port Gibson's last Jews to save it from being torn down and replaced with an asphalt annex to the gas station. The Lumms have restored their unique building and proudly show it to all visitors.

Up in Tennessee, my assistant Max and I spent a Shabbat in his hometown of Memphis, at the Baron Hirsch synagogue. The congregation goes back a long way, but they have moved with their congregants to the suburbs and left the original building behind. This is the case in many American communities—which sometimes made it difficult to find suitable architectural subjects for this book in the United States.

But north of the border, in Canada, I found some interesting synagogues. I had seen photographs of destroyed wooden synagogues and the abandoned or dilapidated buildings that survive in Eastern Europe, in what was once a thriving center of European Jewish culture. Though the architecture of the Canadian synagogues is in no way similar, the decorative motifs echo all the way from Minsk and Pinsk to Toronto and Montreal.

Be strong as a leopard, light as an eagle, swift as a deer and courageous as a lion to do the will of your Father in the Heavens.

—Pirkei Avot 4

This verse inspired many Jewish artists, and became a major pictorial theme in Ashkenazi synagogues in Eastern and Central Europe. It was also the inspiration of the billboard painter who embellished the walls of Toronto's congregation Knesset Israel (Gathering of Israel) with depictions of each of these animals. The setting is theatrical, but the exterior of this plain brick synagogue in a working-class neighborhood gives no hint of its elaborate interior or the origin of its members. The synagogue is located in an area known as Junction, adjacent to the railroad yards. Every passing train rattled my camera.

Exterior, Temple B'nei Israel, Natchez, Mississippi (right)

Memorial ceremony for Israel's fallen, Park East Synagogue, New York City (below)

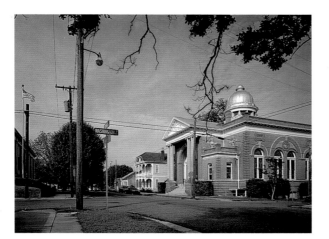

THE CARIBBEAN

SHAAR HASHAMAYIM
SYNAGOGUE, KINGSTON,
JAMAICA, WEST INDIES

BIMAH, *NIDHE YISRAEL*
SYNAGOGUE, BRIDGETOWN,
BARBADOS, WEST INDIES *(opposite)*

NIDHE YISRAEL SYNAGOGUE,
BRIDGETOWN,
BARBADOS, WEST INDIES

ARON KODESH,
NIDHE YISRAEL SYNAGOGUE,
BRIDGETOWN, BARBADOS,
WEST INDIES

ברוך אתה בבאך

ENTRANCE,
MIKVEH ISRAEL-EMANUEL SYNAGOGUE,
WILLEMSTAD, CURAÇAO, WEST INDIES

BANISTER OF BIMAH,
MIKVEH ISRAEL-EMANUEL
SYNAGOGUE, WILLEMSTAD,
CURAÇAO, WEST INDIES
(above left)

BANCA (MEN'S SECTION),
MIKVEH ISRAEL-EMANUEL
SYNAGOGUE, WILLEMSTAD,
CURAÇAO, WEST INDIES
(above right)

MIKVEH ISRAEL-EMANUEL
SYNAGOGUE, WILLEMSTAD,
CURAÇAO, WEST INDIES
(opposite)

UNITED
STATES

TEMPLE
GEMILUTH CHESSED,
PORT GIBSON,
MISSISSIPPI, U.S.A.

TEMPLE
GEMILUTH CHESSED,
PORT GIBSON,
MISSISSIPPI, U.S.A.

TEMPLE B'NAI SHALOM,
BROOKHAVEN,
MISSISSIPPI, U.S.A.
(opposite top)

INTERIOR,
TEMPLE B'NAI SHALOM,
BROOKHAVEN,
MISSISSIPPI, U.S.A.
(opposite bottom)

TEMPLE BETH EL,
LEXINGTON,
MISSISSIPPI, U.S.A.

ANSHE SFARD SYNAGOGUE,
NEW ORLEANS,
LOUISIANA, U.S.A. *(opposite)*

ADATH ISRAEL SYNAGOGUE,
BROWNSVILLE,
TENNESSEE, U.S.A.

*CONGREGATION
MIKVEH ISRAEL,
SAVANNAH,
GEORGIA, U.S.A.*

*TOURO SYNAGOGUE,
NEWPORT,
RHODE ISLAND, U.S.A.*

BIMAH *AND* ARON KODESH,
TOURO SYNAGOGUE,
NEWPORT,
RHODE ISLAND, U.S.A.

TOURO SYNAGOGUE,
NEWPORT,
RHODE ISLAND, U.S.A.

ELDRIDGE STREET
SYNAGOGUE,
NEW YORK CITY,
U.S.A. *(opposite)*

BIALYSTOKER
SYNAGOGUE,
NEW YORK CITY,
U.S.A. *(above)*

CANADA

HAMILTON, ONTARIO,
CANADA (above)

KNESSET ISRAEL
SYNAGOGUE,
TORONTO, ONTARIO,
CANADA (opposite)

KNESSET ISRAEL
SYNAGOGUE,
TORONTO, ONTARIO,
CANADA (top and bottom)

TEMPLE SOLOMON,
MONTREAL, CANADA
(opposite)

NORTHERN EUROPE
ENGLAND, HOLLAND, FRANCE, AND GERMANY

The interior of the Spanish-Portuguese Synagogue in Amsterdam is a hard space to grasp. There is nothing there on which the eye can rest easily—no colored windows, no single decorative element. Although it was built in 1675, it looked more modern than any synagogue I had yet photographed. Dark wood benches filled the entire space, a candle-holder rested behind each seat. Even today, there are no electric lights and no heat in the building: the synagogue is as it was.

At a loss after spending some time there, I went off to the Rijksmuseum to look at architectural

BIMAH, *PLYMOUTH HEBREW CONGREGATION, PLYMOUTH, ENGLAND (left)*

EZRAT NASHIM, PLYMOUTH HEBREW CONGREGATION, PLYMOUTH, ENGLAND (above)

paintings of the period, hoping for inspiration. There I saw paintings of interior spaces that were pulled back, almost cold in their outlook. The painters, though, had placed prominent objects in the foreground or at the side of the scenes, often in subdued tones, in order to allow the viewer into the picture. This is what I tried to do in my own photographs. The light in the synagogue was warm and rich, but now it was so cold that even the air inside seemed hazy and blue; the space was far too large for us even to consider lighting it ourselves. Toward the afternoon of the second day of work, when I had finally decided how to approach the spatial and compositional problems, the sun shone just brightly enough to add some highlights and brighten the room.

I asked the secretary of the congregation how their collection of Judaica had survived the war. He told me that just before the Germans entered Amsterdam, a few members of the congregation had secretly entered and stowed the collection high up on the meter-wide rafters of the ceiling, where they could not possibly be seen from below—the collection remained untouched throughout the war.

In England, I concentrated on the early Ashkenazi synagogues in Exeter and Plymouth. Exeter's small synagogue now serves a membership of about forty people. The Jewish community there may be able to trace its roots as far back as Roman times, but certainly to the Middle Ages. The entire English Jewish community was expelled in 1290 and Jews weren't permitted to dwell in Britain for hundreds of years, until the 1700s. The Exeter synagogue was consecrated in 1764, slightly later than the Plymouth Hebrew Congregation synagogue.

Plymouth's synagogue is a freestanding brick building that looks as if it has been significantly remodeled and restored on the exterior. The interior is a moderately large space dominated by an Italian-style *aron* and a large but simple wooden *bimah* in the center of the room. The feeling is one of light, simplicity of design, and rich tradition. We were met by a representative of the

community, Mr. Greenberg, who told us that the synagogue's membership has dwindled and that they rarely have a quorum for prayer services. Mr. Greenberg conducts tours of school groups; one group of girls came to visit while we were working at the synagogue. He startled me by asking how many of them had heard that Jews have horns. A few hands went up. And then he proceeded to tell them a little bit about Judaism and the synagogue they were in.

In France, I began with Provence. The most important of the Jewish communities in Provence were the four that came to be known as the Four Holy Communities: Avignon, Cavaillon, Carpentras, and Îles-sur-Sorgue. To the west lay the Jewish communities of Languedoc, among them Béziers, Montpellier, and Perpignan. And of course there were Jewish communities to the north, in the area controlled by the Crown; but Provence, for the Gentiles as well as the Jews, was independent and unique.

As you drive through the Provençal countryside in the springtime, these are the colors that you see: the pale, yellowish soil covered with row after row

Mr. Greenberg guiding tour, Plymouth Hebrew Congregation, Plymouth, England

of grapevines; orchards and fields of lavender, all bathed in a soft, warm light; gentle hills dotted with olive trees, and sometimes all of this together—this is the beauty of Provence.

In the Cavaillon synagogue, there is some echo of these colors in the pastel tones of the lushly decorated interior. The porch and entrance to this synagogue are behind a metal gate and fence overlooking the courtyard of the home that used to belong to the rabbi. This building, too, is under restoration. The arrangement of the synagogue is unique. It is a narrow space, with the *aron* located in the middle of the longer wall and a raised platform for the reader's table opposite at the top of a spiral staircase. The decor in Cavaillon is almost frivolous, typical of architecture in Provence in 1772, when it was built. Below the synagogue is a room that contains an oven for baking Passover matzos, which now serves as display space for the Jewish museum.

We made our way later to Paris, where I hoped to photograph two synagogues. One is in the old Jewish quarter known to the Jews of Paris as the Pletzel, on Rue Pavée. It is an Art Nouveau building designed by the well-known architect Hector Guimard.

The synagogue retains a very active congregation, under the guidance of Rav Rottenberg and his son, with whom I was once privileged to have Shabbat meals; they are an extremely hospitable congregation of very kind, very religious people.

In photographing the interior of this space, I chose to do something a little different: to focus on the colorful prayer stand used by the reader during prayer services. We were able to do a very soft and delicately lit photograph, but it took us hours to set up and we worked into the early hours of the morning. There were some dozen men there who were staying up studying Torah; when they needed a break, they would come and sit with us. I overheard one of them say to his friend, "Look how hard they are working in order to make just one perfect photograph. If each of us worked that hard to perfect our mitzvot, the fulfillment of God's commandments, think what we could achieve." I have

Courtyard of former rabbi's home in ghetto, Cavaillon, France (above)

M. Le Rabbin Torjman, Rue Nazareth Synagogue, Paris, France (right)

tried to take those words to heart and make my mitzvot as luminous as this image, but this is a demanding task.

In Germany, I followed the advice of my friend, the photojournalist Tim Gidal, who suggested that I go to Augsburg and see the newly restored synagogue and Jewish museum. So I went there, saw the museum, and showed my work to Senator Julius Spokojny.

Julius Spokojny, originally from Poland, had found himself in Munich after the war. What made Poland a better place for a Jew than Germany? He wanted only to go to Israel and became involved with the Zionist groups who were helping Jews reach Israel's shores. When his wife became pregnant, they couldn't make the journey, and he resigned himself to living in Germany. He told me later that he had spent many nights in the ruined synagogue of Augsburg, along with many other Jewish war refugees. The synagogue was completed in 1917, designed by an architect by the name of Landauer, himself from southern Germany. Imagine—the Jews felt so confident of their status in German society that they completed this opulent structure as Germany itself was being humiliated by the terms of the surrender it was forced to sign following World War I. On Kristallnacht, the evening of November 9, 1938, when all the synagogues of Germany were burned, this synagogue was not completely destroyed. The shell remained and served the Nazis as a stable. Thousands of Jews in the area were later rounded up, and many of them were sent to the nearby concentration camp at Dachau and from there to death camps. Only a few have survived the war, and among the handful of Jews that I met in Augsburg, I don't think any of them had their roots there.

Spokojny told me that, as he lay nightly on the floor and benches of the ruined synagogue, looking up through the enormous dome that now offered no shelter from the rain and cold, he made a vow: if he survived these hard years and could rebuild his life, he would restore this synagogue to its original glory. I questioned him: the people were annihilated—what was the purpose of a synagogue, if no one survived to use it? "The Germans didn't relate to the Jews as human beings, we were to them like rats," he declared. He wanted to remind them that the people they had destroyed were not only human, but people of culture and ability, capable of building magnificent edifices such as this. The synagogue functions now as a museum. School groups come through constantly. I have seen more than one German come in, sit down, and cry.

The Jewish community of Augsburg probably dates back to the Roman period, but this does not mean that the Jews dwelled in peace and security from ancient times until

Prayer stand, Rue Pavée Synagogue, Paris, France

the rise of Hitler. They were subject to the same tribulations suffered by other Jewish communities in Europe, including expulsions, blood libels, and special edicts governing their dress and movement and restricting their religious and economic activity. Hitler introduced no new persecutions; he merely combined all the traditional humiliations together in one short period of the twentieth century. Why then did Jews remain in these Christian countries, which despite periods of relative tolerance were more like death traps? They had few options: there were not many places for them to go, so when they were slaughtered or expelled from one area, they fled to the next available refuge. In the end, they often returned to their original residences, enticed back by a ruler who may have regretted the loss of tax revenues. After the emancipation of European Jewry from most of the strictures that bound them, they were accepted as full citizens. Many of the "enlightened" Jews thought of themselves as representing a synthesis that was distinctly German-Jewish. They felt their place in German society was secure.

Jerusalem motif, Horb Synagogue, Germany, (collection of Israel Museum) (below)

Ezrat Nashim, Augsburg, Germany (right)

For me, the symbol of this synthesis in the Augsburg synagogue are the two large sculptures of griffins, winged lions with the faces of eagles, each standing beside a menorah. The sculptures project amazing stability and power as their enormous claws grip the base of the seven-branched menorahs.

Daniel had a dream . . . as he lay upon his bed . . . the four winds of the heaven stirred up the great sea. And four great beasts came up from the sea . . . The first was like a lion and had eagle's wings. . . .
—Daniel 7:4

The griffin makes its appearance in the Book of Daniel as one of four creatures that symbolize the four major world powers responsible for Israel's devastation and exile from the Land of Israel. The griffin of Daniel is, according to most commentators, a symbol for Babylon, whose armies destroyed the First Temple in Jerusalem. The creature is also the synthesis of the national symbol of Germany, the eagle, and the national symbol of Israel, the Lion of Judah. But for all its grace and power, this strange creature existed only in the imaginations of German Jews. Viewed from the side, these griffins looked almost comforting. Viewed straight on, their faces evince a terrifying cruelty. After that first trip to Augsburg, I was obsessed with Germany, Augsburg, and the Holocaust. The building has been restored to its original glory. But it is no longer a synagogue, it is a sepulchre, a cold and cavernous tomb for the thousand Jews it had once held. Of the synagogues that I have been photographing for the last few years, I like the simple, humble spaces best. But of all the buildings that I have seen that were designed to inspire awe, Augsburg is the most effective—it is, literally, awesome, in the original sense of "inspiring fear"—a place designed to make a man feel small before God.

And now Israel, what does the Lord require of you, but to fear the Lord your God, to walk in all His paths, and to love Him, and to serve the Lord your God with all your heart and all your soul. . . .
—Deuteronomy 10:12–13

ENGLAND

PLYMOUTH HEBREW
CONGREGATION,
PLYMOUTH, ENGLAND

EXETER HEBREW
CONGREGATION,
EXETER, ENGLAND

HOLLAND

STAND FOR PARNASSIM,
SPANISH-PORTUGUESE SYNAGOGUE,
AMSTERDAM, HOLLAND

VIEW TO ENTRANCE,
SPANISH-PORTUGUESE SYNAGOGUE,
AMSTERDAM, HOLLAND *(opposite)*

*VIEW TO TEVAH,
SPANISH-
PORTUGUESE
SYNAGOGUE,
AMSTERDAM,
HOLLAND*

FRANCE

RUE PAVÉE SYNAGOGUE,
PARIS, FRANCE (above)

RUE NAZARETH SYNAGOGUE,
PARIS, FRANCE (opposite)

HEKHAL,
RUE NAZARETH SYNAGOGUE,
PARIS, FRANCE

CAVAILLON, FRANCE
(top)

BIMAH,
CAVAILLON, FRANCE
(bottom)

SYNAGOGUE AT DUSK,
CAVAILLON, FRANCE

GERMANY

NER TAMID
(ETERNAL LIGHT),
AUGSBURG, GERMANY
(top)

MOSAIC, ARON KODESH,
AUGSBURG, GERMANY
(bottom)

READER'S STAND
AND ARON KODESH,
AUGSBURG, GERMANY
(opposite)

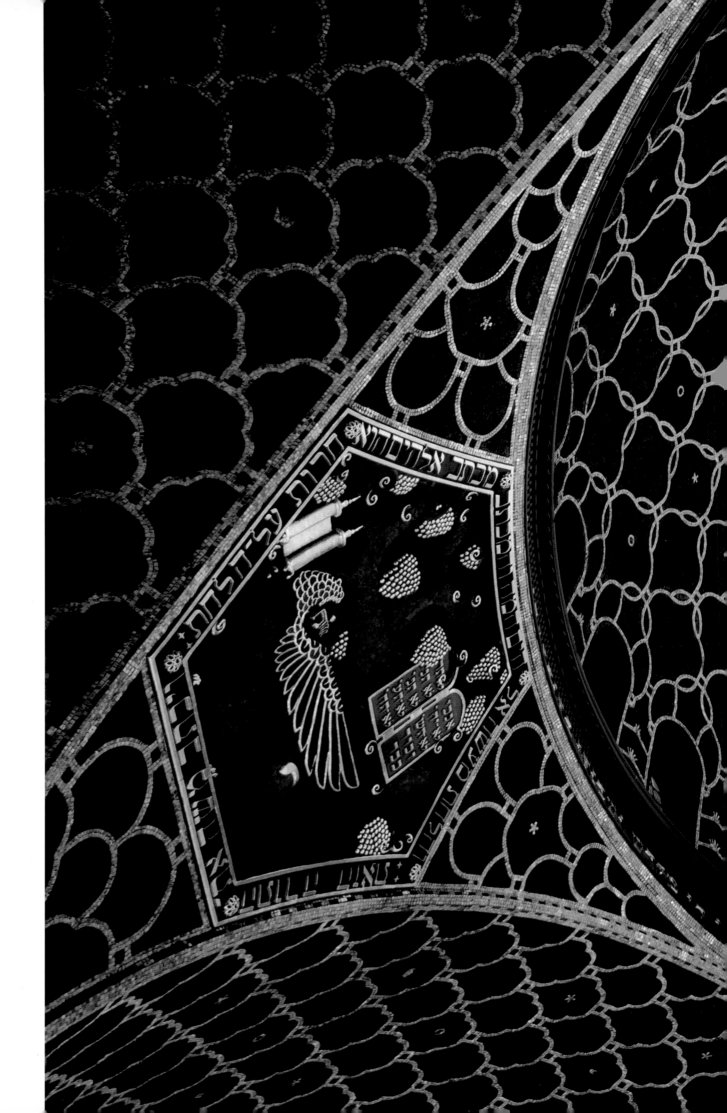

AUGSBURG,
GERMANY

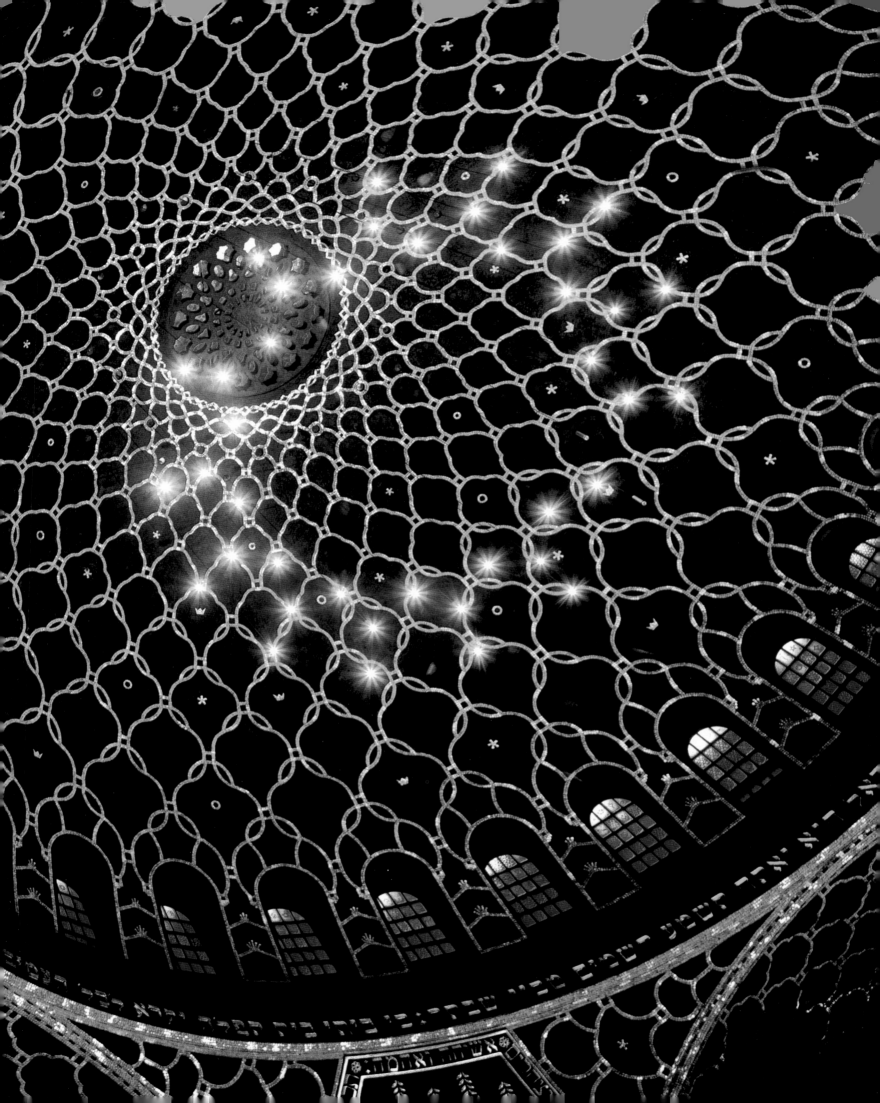

GRIFFIN MENORAH,
AUGSBURG, GERMANY

WOODEN CEILING
OF HORB SYNAGOGUE,
GERMANY (COLLECTION
OF ISRAEL MUSEUM)
(opposite)

EASTERN EUROPE
POLAND, HUNGARY, AND THE CZECH REPUBLIC

Come and see how beloved Israel is of the Holy One, Blessed be He. For every place they were exiled, the Divine Presence is with them. They were exiled to Egypt, and the Divine Presence was with them. . . . They were exiled to Babylon, and the Divine Presence was with them. And when they will be redeemed, the Divine Presence will be redeemed with them. . . .
—Talmud Bavli, Tractate Megilah

The synagogue in Szeged, Hungary—just north of the former Yugoslav border—was built after the Emancipation, at a time when Jews were permitted to build large, freestanding buildings. This one occupies a city block, on a site surrounded by a large iron fence and trees. The interior was built on the same grand scale as the synagogue in Augsburg, but there is more light and the ornamental treatment is more playful at Szeged. This building may not have been the great-

*EXTERIOR, DESTROYED SYNAGOGUE,
RYMANOW, POLAND (left)*

FORMER BEIT MIDRASH FROM SYNAGOGUE, TYKOCIN, POLAND (above)

POLAND

WALL INSCRIPTIONS,
TYKOCIN, POLAND

INTERIOR,
DESTROYED SYNAGOGUE,
RYMANOW, POLAND
(opposite)

TYKOCIN, POLAND (top)

*STARA SYNAGOGUE,
CRACOW, POLAND
(bottom)*

*INTERIOR,
STARA SYNAGOGUE,
CRACOW, POLAND
(opposite)*

LANCUT, POLAND

LANCUT, POLAND

MAD, HUNGARY

MAD, HUNGARY

BALCONIES, PECS,
HUNGARY (above left)

UNDER SOUTH BALCONY,
PECS, HUNGARY
(above right)

NORTH BALCONIES,
PECS, HUNGARY
(opposite)

SZEGED, HUNGARY

THORN AND THISTLE, SZEGED, HUNGARY (top)

DOOR AND BALCONY, SZEGED, HUNGARY (bottom)

SZEGED, HUNGARY (opposite)

SZEGED, HUNGARY

THE CZECH REPUBLIC

ARON KODESH,
ALTNEUSHUL, PRAGUE,
CZECH REPUBLIC (above)

ALTNEUSHUL, PRAGUE,
CZECH REPUBLIC
(opposite)

ISRAEL

One who stands in prayer outside of Israel, should turn his thoughts towards Israel . . . one who prays in Israel, should turn his thoughts towards Jerusalem . . . one who prays in Jerusalem, should turn his thoughts towards the Temple . . . one who prays in the Temple, should turn his thoughts towards the Holy of Holies. . . . Thus, all Israel turn their hearts to a single place.
—Talmud Bavli, Brachot

Over the past two thousand years, this has been an effective manner of keeping Israel and Jerusalem alive in the hearts of the Jewish people. But it means different things to different people: the nonreligious see in Israel a haven free of oppression where the nation— as distinct from the religion—can develop naturally. The religious see Israel as the place where we will

ANCIENT SYNAGOGUE OF BAR AM,
BAR AM, ISRAEL (left)
CARVED STONE DOOR, BAR AM, ISRAEL (above)

achieve both physical and spiritual redemption. I count myself among the religious, and I am a Zionist; that is, I believe that by enhancing the physical connection between the land of Israel and the people of Israel, we will advance our spiritual state as well.

The oldest synagogue that I photographed for this book is the third-century synagogue of Bar Am, located just a few kilometers south of the Lebanese border. It is on a hill bristling with cactus, and on a late summer afternoon, you will often find a Druse family there—while the children play among the ruins of the ancient Jewish village, their parents pick cactus fruit. There are clusters of trees around the site, and next to the eastern wall of the synagogue grow pomegranate and olive trees. Over the crest of the hill are the ruins of the village, and almost at the top of the hill is a small church, which is abandoned. Most days, you can hear the thud of distant firing coming from the direction of Lebanon.

When the synagogue was built it was an impressive building, two stories high with a pitched roof and an arched, stone doorway decorated with fine carvings. The entrance of the building faces south, in the direction of Jerusalem. To enter the building one has to pass first through a colonnade and then through the arched doorway.

Happy is the man who listens to me and is at my gates daily. . . .

—Proverbs 8:34

The Talmud, which was compiled around the same period during which this village was active, interprets this verse to mean that to enter a synagogue one should pass first through an outer and then an inner door. Nowadays, only the facade of this building is more or less complete; the roof is gone and the other walls have crumbled. It is no longer impressive, though many charming details remain.

At night, the synagogue walls stand against the dark starry sky, and it becomes hard to tell where they stop and the sky begins. The building seems whole again, and the columns that stand so awkwardly during the day take on grander dimensions. I stood there one night thinking that the synagogue was more intriguing in the darkness, when one might imagine it as it once was. It seemed logical, then, to photograph it at night using the only type of illumination that would have been available in the third century: torches and candles.

We painted the building with the light of a torch, using a long exposure, while the full moon hovered over the distant lights of the nearby Kibbutz Bar-Am. The synagogue looks like fire itself in this photograph, glowing red like an ancient star that grows ever more distant.

On a lightly wooded hillside in Safed in the upper Galilee, above a deep wadi filled with flowing water and fruit trees, there are several synagogues whose origins date back to the sixteenth century. The synagogues were reconstructed after an earthquake in the 1830s and they stand today, still in use by the Jewish community of Safed. Now the town has grown to cover the entire hill and neighboring hills and valleys.

Today, a stroll through the old city of Safed is a bit like wandering through the stacks of a library: narrow buildings are lined up next to one another like books on a shelf. The buildings, though, rise and fall with the contours of the land; one catches sight of recognizable names on crudely lettered signs, names of Hebrew sages such as Karo, Abuhav, Alsheikh, or the Ari. These names are more often found on the spine of a Hebrew book, but in Safed they are more than names, they are personalities and places—each of these sages has a physical presence here today, a synagogue named for him.

None of these synagogues is exactly as it was, but some of the original color remains. The oldest is the one that used to be named for Elijah the prophet, but was later renamed for Rabbi Isaac Luria, called the Ari, the most famous of the cabalistic sages. This synagogue sits above the graveyard at the bottom of the old city. There used to be a lovely courtyard there with a large fig tree, but now the space has been spoiled by the construction of a large building behind it. I am fortunate to have photographed this courtyard and the interior of the synagogue many years ago. The synagogue is used by the Sephardi community of Safed, and is called the Ari Sephardi—to differentiate it from the one up the hill, called the Ari Ashkenazi. The Ari Ashkenazi was never used by the Ari; it was built in the eighteenth century on the site where he and his students used to go to receive the Sabbath. It too was destroyed and rebuilt after the 1837 earthquake.

The fifteenth-century sage Rabbi Yitzhak Abuhav never reached Safed but he did send a Torah scroll

Jew of Moroccan origin praying at the Western Wall, Jerusalem, Israel (right, above)

Raising of the Torah at the Western Wall, Jerusalem, Israel (right)

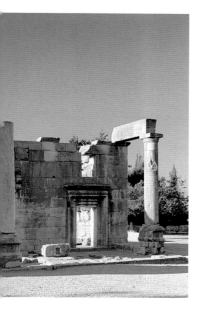

*Facade of synagogue,
Bar Am, Israel (above)*

*Menorah from an ancient
home in the Jewish quarter,
Israel Museum,
Jerusalem, Israel (left)*

with instructions to build a synagogue there. The original building was destroyed in the earthquake, but the Torah scroll was undamaged and the building was rebuilt within a short period. The furniture is made from plain wood painted blue, and the paintings that adorn it are crude but fetching. I photographed it years ago, before they added bright blue plastic chairs to the wooden benches. The Ari synagogue has now become a popular tourist site, so the best time to see it is at the daily prayer service that begins just before sunrise.

Even without these synagogues, Safed would still feel holy. Perhaps it is the clear mountain atmosphere and the narrow lanes that look old and a little neglected, with the implication that the physical aspect is not really important.

The old road between Tel-Aviv and Jerusalem passes by the Mikveh Israel Synagogue. From the highway, a straight road shaded on both sides by towering palms leads directly to it, and beyond to the school. The synagogue is a large stone building. Like all the synagogues that I have seen from this period, the interior is simple. Two rows of arches divide the space. The *aron kodesh* is made of wood painted blue, and the original benches and fixtures have been replaced with newer ones, but these, too, are made of unadorned wood. These places have the spartan feel of the frontier, where there was no money or energy to be wasted on superfluous embellishments. The only decorations are the colored windows and the blue-painted stripes on the ceiling, but the synagogue is appealing for its very simplicity.

The earliest Jewish agricultural settlements in Israel included Zichron Ya'akov in the northern coastal area, and Rishon LeZion in the central part of the country. Production of wine became one of the primary industries in each of these places, industries that flourish there to this day. Both were founded in the 1880s, when the synagogues were constructed. Rishon LeZion (first in Zion) is just down the road from Mikveh Israel, and like it, the Rishon LeZion synagogue building occupies the prime site, in this case at the head of the hill on which the main boulevard was built. At the bottom of the hill stands the old winery. The boulevard ends at the synagogue's entrance.

In Zichron, the synagogue is located in the central square of the town. Both are simple structures with plain facades. The synagogue in Zichron has an elaborately painted interior. Most of the young religious families have by now moved out of the center of the town, but the synagogue continues to be used and maintained by the community. The synagogues of this era are infused with light and an air of optimism born of idealism.

An astonishing conversation took place nearly two millennia ago. It is recorded in the Talmud Bavli Makot 24, that Rabbis Gamliel, Elazar ben Azarya, Yehoshua, and Akiva went together to Jerusalem. From Mount Scopus, they looked down upon the ruins of the Temple, and tore their clothing in a gesture of mourning. When they came to the Temple Mount, they saw a fox leaving the place of the Holy of Holies, and they all wept—except for Rabbi Akiva, who laughed. They asked him why he laughed, to which he responded, "Why are you crying?"

The other rabbis reminded Akiva that, as prophesied, the Temple had fallen into ruins. "Should we not cry?" they exclaimed.

Akiva said, "That is just why I'm laughing." He explained that, while the prophet Uriah said that "Zion will be ploughed up like a field and Jerusalem will be reduced to rubble" (Micah 3:12), Zechariah later predicted (Zechariah 8:4) that "Old men and women will again sit in the streets of Jerusalem . . . and the streets of the city will be filled with playing children."

Akiva continued, "Until I saw the prophecy of Uriah fulfilled, I was afraid that the prophecy of Zechariah would never be realized. Now that I have seen the first come true, there is no doubt about Zechariah's prophecy!"

The other men said to him, "Akiva, you have comforted us. Akiva, you have brought us great comfort!"

What is so extraordinary about this exchange is Akiva's hopefulness in the face of the horrific reality before him: the streets of Jerusalem had been filled with Jewish corpses and most of the survivors had been taken into slavery. Today, Akiva might have been labeled a religious fanatic, unable to face the sad truth surrounding him. But the wisdom and comfort he gave his colleagues long ago has sustained our people to this day.

ARI SYNAGOGUE,
SAFED, ISRAEL

ADES SYNAGOGUE,
JERUSALEM, ISRAEL
(opposite)

*ARI SYNAGOGUE,
SAFED, ISRAEL (top)*

*WESTERN FACADE,
MIKVEH ISRAEL SYNAGOGUE,
ISRAEL (bottom)*

MIKVEH ISRAEL
SYNAGOGUE, ISRAEL

JOHANAN BEN-ZACCAI
SYNAGOGUE,
JERUSALEM, ISRAEL

את בני ישראל

ARI ASHKENAZI   DETAIL OF ARON,
SYNAGOGUE,   ARI ASHKENAZI
SAFED, ISRAEL   SYNAGOGUE,
(opposite)   SAFED, ISRAEL (above)

ZICHRON YA'AKOV,
ISRAEL (above)

ABUHAV SYNAGOGUE,
SAFED, ISRAEL (opposite)

JEW OF MOROCCAN
ORIGIN PRAYING AT THE
WESTERN WALL ON
HOSHANNAH RABBAH,
JERUSALEM, ISRAEL

THE SYNAGOGUE THROUGHOUT THE AGES

YOM TOV ASSIS

A MINIATURE TEMPLE:
THE ORIGINS OF THE SYNAGOGUE

In 70 C.E., when Jerusalem was under siege and about to fall into the hands of Vespasianus, the future emperor of Rome, Johanan ben Zaccai, a renowned scholar of the city, asked his disciples to smuggle him outside the walls in a coffin so that he could appear before the Roman commander. There, he asked permission to establish an academy at Jabneh.[1] A leader who abandoned the besieged capital and its struggling defenders must have shocked and disgusted many of his compatriots; no doubt some of them considered Rabbi Johanan a traitor. Yet in Jewish tradition, neither his action nor his status has ever been questioned, neither his foresight nor his wisdom ever doubted: the academy at Jabneh proved far more vital and lasting than the Temple in Jerusalem.

Perhaps the founder of Jabneh was inspired by a sister institution, closely linked to the academy, that had come into being probably about six centuries earlier, with the destruction of the First Temple by Nebuchadnezzar in 586 B.C.E. and the ensuing Babylonian Captivity. Until then, the Jews had not insisted on the connection between the human need to pray and the erection of a special building; there is evidence that people in ancient Israel prayed anywhere decent, particularly in public squares in the open air. In fact, since the Temple in Jerusalem represented not only the unity of the people but a monotheistic theology that rejected multiple gods and temples, Israelites were forbidden to build temples outside that city. The use of the terms "houses of the people" and "meeting place of God" in the Hebrew Bible fails to prove that synagogues existed in Israel before the Babylonian Captivity.[2] Prayers were recited in various private and public localities, of which the Temple was certainly one. (Several biblical passages indicate that prayers were regularly recited in the Temple, which is called, in one instance, a house of prayer.)[3]

Persistent traditions date the foundation of the synagogue to the early days of the Babylonian Captivity. Some scholars believe that the synagogue came into being in Babylon, where the exiled Jews felt the need to pray and study together in a place of their own. Since they could no longer hold services in public places, the need for a house of worship was natural.

Early Jewish sources generally interpret the prophet Ezekiel's words, "a miniature temple," uttered in Babylon, as referring to a house of worship and study.[4] According to a Talmudic tradition, some synagogues in Babylon have existed since the Babylonian Captivity.[5]

The Jews who settled in Egypt and other parts of North Africa around the period of the destruction of the First Temple, in 586 B.C.E., built temples, but this was never the norm in the Diaspora, where the synagogue became the center of Jewish life and the sole house of worship. Although the first conclusive evidence of the existence of synagogues comes from the Hellenistic Egypt of the third century B.C.E., it is unlikely that the synagogue originated there. If the synagogue did not exist in Israel before the destruction of the First Temple, it was either brought back from the Captivity by Jews returning to their homeland after 538 B.C.E., or founded in the Land of Israel about the same period.

In the century before the destruction of the Second Temple, numerous synagogues existed in Israel and in the Diaspora. The synagogue became so well established as a religious institution that there was even one in the precincts of the Temple itself. The general population of Israel came to be divided into twenty-four groups, their representatives being sent to the Temple in weekly rotation; during the week, the members of the group who remained behind gathered in the local synagogue, where they prayed and read from the Bible. Ancient sources testify to the order of service in the synagogue within the Temple on the Day of Atonement: at that time, sacrifices and prayers existed side by side.[6]

With the destruction of the Second Temple, in 70 C.E., the synagogue with the *beth midrash* (or academy) on its premises became the center of Jewish life. The anniversary of the destruction was a day of mourning and fasting for generations, but the Jews survived the disaster and Judaism adapted itself successfully to the new conditions of life without a homeland and without a temple. If the Torah was the Jews' portable homeland in their long sojourn in exile, the synagogue as a house of worship and study was indeed their miniature temple, and their most vital institution. Wherever a Jewish community came into being, a synagogue was established. Indeed no Jewish community, however modest, existed without one.

SYNAGOGUE RITUAL AND LITURGY

An old tradition attributes the first formulation of Jewish prayers in public to the men of the Great Synod, an institution of the Second Temple period. The earliest prayers are associated with Ezra and Nehemiah, the two leaders from Babylon, who led the rebuilding of the Second Jewish Commonwealth in the fifth century B.C.E. These prayers consisted of two parts: the three passages from the Torah known as the *Shema'*, with the appropriate blessings, and the *'Amidah* or Eighteen Benedictions, the Jewish prayer par excellence. The formulation of set prayers was not universally accepted without opposition, but an order of prayer became the norm in synagogues long before the destruction of the Second Temple. *The Mishnah*, edited around 200 C.E., includes important information from earlier centuries on prayers recited in public with a quorum of at least ten adult men. The antiquity of the main prayers explains their inclusion in the earliest rituals that developed in Israel and Babylon.[7]

From these two centers of Jewry, Israel and Babylon, different rituals grew and spread throughout the Diaspora. In certain periods these branches of ritual coexisted in the two centers and in different countries. The original forms of each branch have not survived, but Talmudic literature allows us more or less to reconstruct them, and the rituals of all subsequent Jewish communities seem to belong to one or the other of the two branches. From the seventh century onward, when the Jews lived under either Islam or Christian power, the two branches of the rituals coincided with the political and religious division of the Jewish world: the rituals of the Israel branch prevailed in Christian lands, while those of Babylon spread in the Muslim world. The influence of the ritual of the Land of Israel in the synagogues of the Christian lands was due to the close links between the Jewish communities in Christendom and in Israel, which was under Byzantine rule until the Arab conquest in 632. The communities under Islam were influenced by the Jewish community in Babylon, which for 500 years, beginning under Abbasid rule in the eighth century, was the center of the Muslim Empire.[8]

The Israel branch of ritual included the Romaniot[9] or Byzantine ritual, the Italian, the French, the German or Ashkenazi, and, closely related to the latter, the Polish. The Romaniot rite was maintained in the Byzantine Empire, and it survived under the Turks in several localities where Greek-speaking Jews were a significant part of the local Jewish population—even remaining the majority when, after 1492, masses of Jewish refugees from Spain settled in the Ottoman Empire. Ioannina, in northern Greece, and Chalkis, north of Athens, remained Romaniot until their almost complete extinction in our own century.[10] In Istanbul, where Romaniots were numerous, several synagogues practicing the Romaniot ritual operated until the beginning of the twentieth century.

The Italian ritual is the most ancient of all the extant rites in the branch, and there are still synagogues that follow it in Rome, Venice, Milan, Padua, and elsewhere in Italy, as well as in the Italian synagogue in Jerusalem. In the past, synagogues using the Italian liturgy could be found in Corfu and Turkey. The ancient French liturgy, as found in the *Mahzor Vitry* and other sources, was once practiced throughout the north of France, and also in England, with the arrival of Norman Jews there after the conquest of 1066. It was lost as a result of a series of expulsions, beginning in 1290 and ending in 1394; closely related to the German ritual, it was absorbed by the latter as French Jews settled in Ashkenazi communities. French Jews were also eventually assimilated within local communities elsewhere, although there were for a time some French synagogues outside France—the Sinagoga de los franceses in Barcelona, for example, where sixty Jewish families from France were allowed to settle after the expulsion of 1306. The French ritual did survive until the twentieth century in three Piedmontese synagogues in northwest Italy, in Asti, Fossano, and Moncalvo. And there are traces of its influence in the liturgy of other Piedmontese synagogues.

The German or Ashkenazi liturgy and its Polish variation are certainly the most widespread of all. Originating in Germany, this ritual spread into Eastern Europe as a result of persecutions and expulsions. Synagogues following the Ashkenazi liturgy were established wherever sufficient numbers of German Jews settled—in Italy, Turkey, Holland, Israel, and in recent times throughout Western Europe and America. The Ashkenazi prayer book contains passages reflecting the history of many of the different communities that have used it.

More than a thousand years of Jewish life in Babylon produced a ritual distinct in many details from the rites of the Israel center. With the Muslim conquests, this tradition spread throughout the lands under Muslim rule. Following the transfer of the political and religious center to Baghdad, Babylonian Jewry was able to propagate its norms and customs in communities scattered throughout the vast Muslim empire. The Abbasid authorities recognized the leadership of the Babylonian academies of Sura and Pumbeditha for all the Jews living within their realm. These academies had already established their prominence in Jewish life over several centuries, and it was convenient for the Abbasid caliph to promote their jurisdiction and influence, as well as the authority of the exilarch (the head of Babylonian Jewry) in all the communities under his rule. The close contacts that Jewish communities in the Islamic world maintained with the academies of Babylon introduced a considerable uniformity in the order of service and the form of prayers. The Babylonian or Oriental prayer book served as a model for communities in the Muslim world.

The Spanish order of prayers is the most obvious example of a ritual of the Babylonian branch. The process through which

Spanish Jewry came within the Babylonian center's sphere of influence can be easily traced. Two instances may illustrate the point: in the middle of the ninth century, Natronai Gaon, head of the academy in Sura, Babylon, was asked by the Jews of Lucena to send them the order of service. He did so, in the brief *Seder Meah Berakhot* (The order of a hundred benedictions). A few years later Amram Gaon, then the head of the same academy, sent a full prayer book at the request of the communities of Spain. This prayer book, known as *Sidur Amram Gaon*, survives.

The Spanish or Sephardi liturgy developed and evolved over time. One distinctive characteristic of it was the religious poetry written during the "Golden Age," between 950 and 1148, by the famous poets of Andalusian Jewry, the best-known among them being Abraham ibn Ezra, Moses ibn Ezra, and Yehudah Halevi. This poetry adorns the Sephardi prayers for the festivals and High Holidays. An additional Sephardi deviation was the profound influence of the Cabala in the late Middle Ages. In time, the Sephardi prayer book became independent of its Babylonian counterpart.

With the Jews' expulsion from Spain, the refugees took their ritual with them. Over time, it divided and subdivided into several variants. Wherever a sufficient number of Jews from the same Spanish town or region settled in the Ottoman Empire, they formed their own congregation and synagogue, where they used their own ritual. Thus the Aragonese and Catalan Jews in Salonika and Edirne had their own synagogues and prayer books, the *Mahzor Aragon* and *Mahzor Barcelona*, which were published in Turkey about three hundred years ago.

Where the Jews of Spain settled, their prayer book often replaced the local one, the native Jews being gradually assimilated within Sephardi Jewry. This occurred in many Middle Eastern and Balkan Romaniot or Greek-speaking, and Oriental or Arabic-speaking communities, and also in North Africa, particularly in Morocco. Some Spanish Jews crossed the border to Portugal in 1492, only to be trapped there and forcibly converted to Christianity in 1497; in the seventeenth century, Jews of this *converso* ancestry established communities in Amsterdam, London, Hamburg, Bayonne, and Bordeaux, and later they arrived in the New World. Leaving Christianity after several generations of crypto-Jewish life, they lacked any tradition of their own, but with the guidance of Sephardi rabbis from established communities of the Sephardi diaspora in the Mediterranean basin, they adopted the ritual in vogue in Italy, Morocco, and the Ottoman Empire, introducing some variants. This is the Spanish and Portuguese ritual prevalent now in London, Amsterdam, New York, and other localities where Western Sephardim live.

The Yemenite ritual is a special branch of the Babylonian group, Yemenite Jewry being one of the most ancient and isolated communities in the Diaspora. Persecutions and oppression in Yemen could have brought despair, had it not been for the guidance, consolation, and inspiration of the twelfth-century Jewish philosopher Maimonides. His comforting words were gratefully acknowledged by the Yemenite Jews, who venerated him and accepted his decisions and customs in all fields, including the order of service. Their prayer book, the Takhlal, was deeply influenced by him. Two rituals eventually emerged in Yemen, one of them the old local ritual, the other the Sephardi-oriented rite.

There was a Persian Jewish ritual that is now found only in manuscript; it was completely overtaken by the Sephardi-Oriental prayer book—the Sephardi prayer book used in the eastern part of the Mediterranean basin. And a Provençal ritual was maintained for centuries in Avignon, Carpentras, Cavaillon, and Île-sur-Sorges. These towns are all in the Comtat Venaissin area, which was part of the Papal States until the French Revolution. When the Jews in the rest of France were finally expelled in 1394, these communities were allowed to exist uninterrupted—the only ones in France to do so. (The first Jews to reappear in France, at the beginning of the seventeenth century, were ex-*conversos* whose first steps in Judaism had been made underground in southwestern France in the latter part of the sixteenth century.) The Provençal ritual belonged definitively to neither the Babylonian nor the Israel branch, and probably contained elements of both. The four Jewish communities of the Comtat Venaissin, which preserved this special liturgy, began to decline rapidly after the French Revolution. Following the emancipation of the Jews, in 1791, the Comtadin Jews were allowed to leave the region and settle anywhere in France. Their assimilation was rapid, although Provençal services were held until World War II. Today the synagogues in Avignon and Carpentras are occupied by recent Jewish immigrants, mostly from North Africa, who hold Sephardi services. The synagogue in Cavaillon is no longer in use and is kept as a museum.[11]

The Sephardi prayer book underwent a radical transformation following the expulsion from Spain. Mysticism spread wide among the refugees, notably in sixteenth-century Safed, in the Galilean mountains of northern Israel, where Sephardi Jews were concentrated. Here, new prayers and other changes were introduced in the service. A whole part was added to the evening service on Friday, the so-called *Kabbalat Shabbal*, which includes the poem "Lekha Dodi," written by one of the Safed mystics, Shelomo HaLevi Alkabets, and now sung on the Sabbath eve in practically every Jewish community in the world. Another great Safed mystic was Joseph Caro, the author of the *Shulhan 'Arukh*, which became the code of law for Jews all over the world. Far the greatest mystic was Isaac Luria, whose brief two-year stay in Safed left a deep impact. He and the other mystics changed both the form and the content of the prayers. And it wasn't the Sephardi prayer book alone that was affected: thanks to rabbis who accepted the Lurianic Cabala, mysticism penetrated deep into Poland. The result was a new ritual among Ashkenazi Jews, the *Sepharad*, which combined the old service with cabalistic passages and Sephardi versions of several prayers. Spreading fast, this ritual became the standard order of service in the Hasidic movement. It spread farther in modern Israel, where some rabbinic authorities have proposed it as the most suitable version of the prayers when people of different backgrounds come to pray together.[12]

THE JEWISH PRAYER—ITS STRUCTURE

To understand the role of the synagogue in Jewish life, it is necessary to know something of the structure of the Jewish prayer, some details of which remain constant in all rituals and in all communities. In principle, the synagogue is the primary place for public prayers—prayers held with the participation of at least ten adult men.

The Jew is expected to recite three prayers a day: morning (*Shahrit*), afternoon (*Minhah*), and evening (*Arvit* or *Maariv*) services. On Sabbaths, festivals, and the new moon (*Rosh Hodesh*) there is an additional service (*Musaf*), and on the Day of Atonement (Yom Kippur), a fifth, concluding service (*Ne'ilah*) is recited. The Jewish prayer consists essentially of the *'Amidah*, which is said silently, standing up, and facing Jerusalem. No interruption or disturbance whatsoever is permitted during the *'Amidah*. In the evening and morning prayers, the *Shema'* is read before the *'Amidah*, and is preceded and followed by benedictions. The *Shema'* consists of three passages from the Torah[13] that contain the Jews' principal beliefs. The first passage begins with the verse "Hear, O Israel, the Lord is our God, the Lord is One," from time immemorial the essence of the Jews' credo.[14]

Another important part of the Jewish prayer is public reading from the Torah, which takes place only in the presence of a quorum of ten men—a minyan. The Torah is read after the *'Amidah* in the morning on Saturdays, festivals, new moons, fast days, and Mondays and Thursdays; it is also read before the *'Amidah* in the afternoon on Saturdays, the Day of Atonement, and fast days. On Saturday mornings the Torah is read in sequence, a portion each week, so that the entire book is completed in the course of a year. The weekly portion is called the *Parashah* or *Sidrah*. This annual cycle, which has spread throughout the Jewish world, originated in Babylon. A triennial cycle was followed in Israel, but was eventually supplanted by the Babylonian custom. On festivals and fast days the passages read from the Torah contain details about the occasion.

As the reading from the Torah was principally meant to fulfill an educational aim, it was sometimes translated into Aramaic during the years when that language was widely used by Jews of the Near East—from the late Second Temple period until the sixth century. The *Turgeman* or translator rendered the Aramaic

(or sometimes the Greek) version of the Torah simultaneously with the Hebrew reading. The custom declined and eventually disappeared as Jews ceased to be familiar with Aramaic and Greek. From the late Second Temple period on, the weekly portion of the Torah was also the subject of a sermon in the synagogue. It was often delivered by the person who read from the scroll of the Torah. In the period following the destruction of the Temple, the sermon became a widespread custom in the synagogue.

Participants were originally expected to read their own portion when they were called up to the Torah, but as the knowledge of Hebrew diminished, a reader was appointed to read on their behalf. The number of people called to the Torah depended on the day: on Saturday seven, on Yom Kippur six, on festivals five, on festive days and on new moons four, and on other occasions three people were invited to read. Except in Reform synagogues, this order remains customary today. Those called up to the Torah have to be adults—at least thirteen years of age. In ancient times, the sources suggest, women could equally be called to the Torah, but this custom was discontinued. In modern times, however, both women and men may be called to the Torah in Reform and some Conservative synagogues.[15]

Traditionally, public prayers can take place only in the presence of a minyan. Ten ordinary, even ignorant men can constitute this quorum for prayer, but nine great scholars cannot. There is evidence that seven men formed a minyan in the Land of Israel, but this custom did not spread. The presence of a minyan allows the prayers to be recited in full. In the absence of a minyan the Torah is not taken from the ark, and no reading of it can take place. Nor does a reader repeat the *'Amidah*, or important parts of the prayers—the kaddish,[16] the *Kedushah*, and the priestly blessing—unless there is a minyan. In various periods, communities have tried different devices to ensure the quorum. In antiquity, communities had *'Asarah Batlanim*, ten men of leisure, present at all times for this purpose. In recent times, communities have hired men for the same goal.

DECORUM AND ATTIRE

The Jew's private prayers are his or her prerogative, and can take place any time and anywhere, including, of course, the synagogue. The synagogue, however, was not established to offer the individual Jew a place to pray to God. Its Hebrew name, *beth knesset*, as well as its Aramaic and Greek names, and through the latter its name in all the European languages, signifies a place of gathering or house of meeting; its function, then, is public. And one of its main functions is the public prayer.

Many ancient sources emphasize the importance of public prayers. "Ten people who pray together, the Divine Presence is with them," says one Talmudic source. Another, "The Holy One Blessed be He is found in the synagogue," connects synagogue and worshipers.[17] The ten men of the minyan, an obligation of assembly that goes back to antiquity, represent the general Jewish public or community, without whom prayers in public cannot take place. Given this communal involvement in prayers, certain rules are necessary for them to be conducted harmoniously. The necessity to meet at least three times a day, at specific times, for example, is a disciplinary measure that eliminates any anarchic tendencies. Several parts of the prayers impose similar demands: the *'Amidah*, for example, must be recited silently and standing up. Similarly, the *Shema'* and its benedictions must be said without unnecessary interruption.

These restrictions aside, however, no strict rules apply to all congregations. And although, in general, the average Jew behaves more or less the same way he does elsewhere, the quality of decorum during the services has never been compatible with their contents. Rabbinic injunctions against improper behavior in the synagogue failed to end practices that were widespread in the ancient Jewish world. The custom, recorded in *The Mishnah*, of pious men spending an hour in meditation before commencing their prayers was an ideal; it was never standard behavior.[18] The same is true of verses such as "I have set the Lord always before me"[19] and the statement "Know before whom you stand," both often found inscribed in synagogues.

Talk during the service, though severely condemned, disturbed rabbis in all countries throughout the Middle Ages. Some medieval communities issued ordinances against worshipers who disturbed their neighbors in prayer and disrupted the service; these ordinances achieved little. Complaints about laughter, chatter, and secular conversation have never ceased. To avoid noise and lack of decorum, Maimonides went as far as omitting the repetition of the *'Amidah* during *Musaf* (the additional service) on Sabbaths and festivals. He was very concerned that irreverent behavior could leave a bad impression on the non-Jewish observer or visitor.

Lack of decorum was not necessarily the result of irreverence or lack of piety: Jews usually felt a certain degree of familiarity in the synagogue. The duration of the prayers, and the use of the synagogue for educational, social, and communal purposes, also contributed to any laxity of conduct during the services. Other disturbances were in any case far more serious. Acts of violence in the synagogue were naturally condemned by rabbis and synagogue officers everywhere, in the medieval world and in modern times. In France and Germany from the eleventh century on, prayers could be interrupted by Jews whose grievances had gone unsatisfied and who wanted to put pressure on a fellow Jew, most likely present in the synagogue, to consent to appear in court or to comply with a court decision. This custom was so abused that it had to be restricted.

Jews are required to be appropriately and cleanly dressed in the synagogue. Their clothes must be Halakhically acceptable. Except in modern times in non-Orthodox synagogues, women cover their heads; in Orthodox and traditionalist synagogues, men do also. The origin of this obligation for men is unclear; there is no reference to it in biblical sources, while the Talmud mentions it as a custom not universally practiced. By the Middle Ages, however, most communities considered covering the head mandatory during prayers. (In Italy and many Sephardi communities, the practice was restricted to prayer.) The custom endured and spread throughout the Jewish world, and was only rejected in modern times by Reform Judaism.

In many communities people had to wash their hands before entering the synagogue. Some synagogues built in the late Middle Ages still hold a special sink for this purpose. People entered the synagogue with clean hands.[20]

MUSIC AND SONG

All Jewish communities sing their prayers to God. It is assumed that what is pleasing to man's ears will be pleasing to God, for in singing, man is offering to God the best he can offer his fellow man. The beginnings of Jewish liturgical music are far from clear, although there must be a link between synagogal music and the musical tradition of the Temple service. We know from various psalms that songs of God were accompanied by musical instruments; we also know that the Temple had an orchestra and choir of Levites. With the destruction of the Temple, however, its musical tradition ended, not only because services were interrupted but also because of self-imposed mourning restrictions. In commemoration of the Temple, musical instruments were prohibited on Saturdays and festivals.

The earliest references to liturgical music date from Talmudic times. The Hazan (the officiating minister) was expected to have a good voice, and his intonation was to instill the right spirit for the occasion, whether joyous or sad, in the hearts of the participants. Musical notes were added to Scriptures, so that they were chanted accordingly. Different cantillations developed for different books and sections of the Bible. Ashkenazim, Sephardim, Romaniots, Arabic-speaking Orientals, Yemenites, Italians, and others have their own tunes for this cantillation; while the musical signs, known as *teamim*, are the same for all communities, the tunes differ among the various branches of Jewry.

From the sixth and seventh centuries onward, with the end of the Talmudic period, the chanting of prayers in the synagogue became the norm. Eventually the Hazan wouldn't just be expected to have a good voice and musical ability, he would be chosen for them. In the Middle East, the music of the Byzantine Christian church left a deep impact on early Jewish liturgical music. Gradually, scholars began to appreciate the value of tunes, and encouraged the embellishment of the prayers with the poems and songs called *piyutim*. It was the *paytanim*, the authors of these liturgical poems, who made the first major contributions to synagogal music. The tunes to the *piyutim*, some of them borrowed from non-Jews, were sometimes indicated in prayer books, and sometimes aroused strong criticism. By then, however, the Jews of the ever-expanding Diaspora no longer knew the ancient musical traditions of Israel. Inevitably, then, synagogal music was deeply influenced by local music, wherever the Jews found themselves.

Taking shape in the Middle Ages, these different musical traditions were incorporated in local Jewish practices—so much so that scholars were known to oppose attempts to deviate from what had become the accepted local tune. The Jewish musical tradition that developed under the impact of local music in Italy offers a good illustration of Jewish people's cultural and social integration in their surroundings. Ashkenazi liturgical music followed the pioneering work of the German Rabbi Jacob Mollin (1356–1427), who collected the traditional tunes with precision and included them in an authoritative liturgical work. In Poland, music had an important place in the synagogue ritual; some songs lasted a long time, and were the subject of both informed and amateur critique. The cantors were given a free hand to compose their own pieces, some of which became integral parts of the repertoire of Ashkenazi Jews in Eastern Europe.

The Jews expelled from Spain brought their songs and music with them, and some of these Iberian tunes have survived until our own day. Similarities in music found in various parts of the Sephardi diaspora—in the Middle East, the Balkans, North Africa, Western Europe—indicate a common Spanish origin. In the Sephardi communities of the Ottoman Empire, the local Oriental or Turkish music gradually came to dominate Jewish liturgical music. The music of the eastern Sephardi synagogues is dominated by the Turkish *maqams*, special melodies or keys, and by Romance tunes of Spanish origin. The Spanish and Portuguese Jews who passed through the *converso* or crypto-Jewish experience, and had to establish their synagogues without any liturgical tradition, introduced Hispano-Christian music to the service, and absorbed tunes introduced by the Sephardi rabbis from Turkey, Morocco, and Italy whom they engaged to guide them in reconstructing their Jewish life.

Until modern times, no choirs accompanied the Hazan or cantor, but many parts of the prayers were sung by the entire congregation. On special occasions, *bahurim* or young singers accompanied the cantor. In Eastern European synagogues this custom disrupted the smooth progress of the service and added little to the musical aesthetics. In some Sephardi synagogues in the Ottoman Empire, *maftirim* or *mezamerim*, members of special choirs, assisted the cantor in the prayers.[21]

The earliest sources referring to synagogues and prayers contain nothing to suggest that a special type of building had to be dedicated or built for the purpose. Any building or part of it could serve as a synagogue. According to one ancient source, however, the synagogue in antiquity had to be in the highest part of the town, and its entrance had to be from the east.[22] Another ancient source determines Jerusalem as the direction of the Jew's prayers, but this rule doesn't seem to have affected the synagogue's position.

The scarcity of sources on the synagogue's architecture is compensated for by the numerous archaeological discoveries of synagogues in Israel and in the Mediterranean basin. For reasons that remain obscure, many of these synagogues were outside their cities. From the third until the seventh centuries C.E., in Galilee and elsewhere in Israel, many synagogues had the same structure: a central hall surrounded by three or four naves. The entrance to these early synagogues was from the same side as the direction of the prayers—in the case of the Galilean synagogues, the southern side, facing Jerusalem. A central entrance with two side doors was most prevalent in these synagogues. Contrary to subsequent developments, these early synagogues had architectural details of animal, vegetal, human, and geometrical figures in mosaic. The zodiac was a common device; there were also such well-known Jewish symbols as the palm-tree branch, the seven-branched candlestick, and the shofar, the ram's-horn trumpet. In some synagogues, scenes of biblical episodes—the sacrifice of Isaac, Daniel and the lions, Noah's ark—adorned the walls. Sometimes the floor was also ornamented with drawings and mosaics. Some of the artists were Jewish, others Gentile. There is evidence that in antiquity there were synagogues without a roof.

Ancient synagogues in the Diaspora had many of the same architectural characteristics of these synagogues in Israel. In Sardis, in Asia Minor, the direction of prayers and the placement of the entrance door were toward Jerusalem. In Ostia, near Rome, the palm-tree branch, the candlestick, and the shofar were engraved on two columns. On the floor of a synagogue in the ancient North African town of Naro (modern Hamam-Lif), not far from Carthage, were mosaics of birds, animals, flowers, and fruit, all of them, an inscription indicates, donated by one Juliana. Most synagogues of antiquity were rectangular, like the great synagogue in Alexandria, which the Talmud describes in picturesque terms.

In time, the straight lines of the basilica of the early period changed to more Gothic or Moorish styles. Both Christianity and Islam, however, imposed restrictions on the size and height of the building. These restrictions were largely upheld throughout the Middle Ages, with several outstanding exceptions. The so-called El Tránsito synagogue of Samuel Halevi

Abulafia, built in 1356 in Toledo, was one of the most impressive buildings in the city. And Toledo's other remaining synagogue, that of Santa Maria la Blanca, was also quite large. These buildings, however, are not representative of medieval synagogues' usually modest size and external architecture. They reflect the high position and large degree of cultural and social integration enjoyed by the Jews of the region, or at least of those who built them. Abulafia's synagogue was in no way compatible with the humiliated status that the Church assigned the Jews.

These Toledo synagogues are in the *mudéjar* style, which reflects the Muslim influence in Christian Spain.[23] The same style is visible in the Córdoba synagogue, and in Segovia's Sinagoga Mayor, which since the fifteenth century has been the Corpus Christi church. Synagogues elsewhere in both Europe and the Muslim world often blended with the local architectural style. The wooden synagogues built in the Slavonic fashion in Poland in the sixteenth and seventeenth centuries contained special Jewish traits, but many medieval synagogues were not originally built as such—the buildings were adapted to the function later. Many late-medieval synagogues hid behind an ordinary facade, and were hardly recognizable from the outside. Only on entering did one realize one was in a synagogue. This is conspicuous in Italian cities such as Venice and Ferrara, in many Piemontese synagogues, in the old synagogues of Izmir, Turkey, and in other places.

A Talmudic dictum states that one should pray only in a place where there are windows.[24] The regulation was applied to synagogues. According to the Zohar, a synagogue should have twelve windows; the *Shulhan 'Arukh* gives the same advice. In early times there was no ark, and the entranceway was the most impressive and important part of the synagogue. When people stood to pray, they faced the entrance, which was oriented toward Jerusalem. When the ark became a fixed and central part of the synagogue, around the fourth century C.E., it was placed at the wall toward Jerusalem, so that prayers were recited as the public stood facing the Torah scrolls. The entrance was now moved either to the opposite wall or to one of the side walls.

Many synagogues had a courtyard or vestibule before the main entrance. Various explanations have been given for this structure, a widely accepted one being that the courtyard is an area where Jews may undergo the necessary spiritual preparation as they pass from the outside world to the realm of prayer and meditation. With its surrounding wall, the courtyard also prevents the services from being exposed to onlookers. Be that as it may, in some countries courtyard and wall met the demands of local authorities that the synagogue's services should not disturb passersby. The courtyard became an important part of synagogue life: children played there, adults chatted, certain services—fast-day services, the benediction for the moon—were recited there. Weather permitting, the courtyard was used for study. Finally, poor people who had no seats prayed outside when the synagogue was full.

This vestibule or forecourt often contained washing facilities. In Muslim lands, in certain communities and periods, Jews under the influence of Islam washed their hands and also their feet there before entering the synagogue hall. The washing of hands alone was more broadly observed; we find a washbasin in the vestibule of many synagogues. Sometimes charity boxes were also placed there, hanging on the wall or set into it. In many Italian synagogues, the washbasins and the charity boxes have survived to this day.

The interior of the synagogue underwent certain changes over time, and different styles developed in different parts of the Diaspora. Some medieval synagogues were in Romanesque or Gothic style, with a double-nave structure and a vaulted roof supported by pillars. Some had a single nave. Most synagogues built as such had columns, which permitted congregants to pray undisturbed by others, and divided the synagogue into areas in which different activities could take place simultaneously.

The ladies' gallery, an integral part of many synagogues in modern times, was not always present in ancient and medieval synagogues. In fact we do not know the exact origins of the separation of men and women in prayer. In the Temple, the *'Ezrat Nashim* or women's sector was not exclusively reserved for women; it was, however, the area beyond which women could not enter. Originally, women seem to have participated fully in the services. In ancient synagogues, the women's quarter was on the same floor and behind the men's. In Babylonian synagogues at one time, there were separate rows for men and women. The galleries found in some ancient synagogues may have been designed for women, but we lack clear evidence.

The situation became more complex in the Middle Ages. In his *Mishne Torah*, in the chapter dealing with the building of the synagogue, Maimonides does not mention a women's section at all. An Ashkenazi scholar of the early thirteenth century, however, tells us that on the Sabbath, a curtain was drawn before the sermon between the men's and women's sections. Gradually a women's room came to be added adjacent to the men's auditorium. In many medieval synagogues this room was a later addition. The term "women's synagogue"—Barcelona's Sinagoga de las dones, for instance—may refer either to the women's room in the synagogue or to a synagogue that contained such a room. In Provence, the women's prayer hall was below the men's auditorium, and the women could only see the Torah scroll through a hole when it was raised for the public to view and kiss from afar. This was the case in Carpentras. The separation between men and women became more rigid toward the late Middle Ages; in the final stage the women prayed behind an opaque screen of glass, wood, or fabric, and women's galleries were constructed in many synagogues. In modern times, some synagogues removed the screens and curtains from the women's galleries. This step was opposed by conservatives, and often led to conflicts in the communities.[25]

THE SYNAGOGUE—ITS FURNITURE AND APPURTENANCES
The type and location of the synagogue's furniture changed no less than its exterior and structure, reflecting a variety of traditions and local influences. The similarities among synagogues of different countries suggest that major prototypes left their impact in large parts of the Diaspora. Whereas the synagogue's exterior was subjected to outside supervision and restrictions, Jews enjoyed almost total freedom in decorating and furnishing the inside.

The ark became the most important part of the synagogue, the congregation's object of reverence. Here the community placed the scrolls of the Torah, which were taken out for the public reading of the Law on Sabbaths, festivals, fast days, and other occasions. The ark was in ancient times called the *tevah*, or "chest," and was portable. It was kept in a room adjacent to the synagogue's main hall, or even in another building altogether (particularly understandable when synagogues were built outside the town), from which it was brought to the service.

Later on, the word "*tevah*" was applied to the permanently installed case in which communities began to place the scroll of the Law. This case, almost invariably set by the wall facing Jerusalem, became the focal point of the synagogue's interior decoration, and of the service itself. In some periods and places a special apse was constructed to contain the ark, which was made, increasingly elaborately, of wood or marble. Some arks are outstanding artworks. In many synagogues the ark was an elevated construction, so that steps were built up to it. The Zohar, the main book of Jewish mysticism, even determined the number of steps.

German, French, and Italian Jews called the ark the "*aron kodesh*," and covered its doors with a *parokhet*, a curtain. The Sephardim of Spain and the Muslim East used the term "*hekhal*"; they too used a curtain, but hung it inside the ark's doors. Lions usually dominated the ornaments on both the *parokhet* and the ark itself; the images of the round-topped tablets of the Law, the Decalogue, that are so widespread in modern synagogues are a relatively recent innovation, of Christian origin. In some areas, such as Piemonte and Provence, the ark was a room that one entered to remove or return the scrolls of the Torah, which were placed on some type of a shelf. In synagogues in Greece, Izmir, and elsewhere, the ark was split into three parts, a central container with two smaller ones on its flanks. The function of this tripartite ark is unclear.

Just as the ark in the synagogue was a substitute for the ark in the Sanctuary[26] and the Temple, so was the *parokhet* a substitute for the curtain found in those religious institutions. Just as the *parokhet* of antiquity separated the Holy of Holies from the rest of the chamber, the *parokhet* in the synagogue of Talmudic times hung at a certain distance from the ark. The curtain was later attached to the doors of the ark, in Ashkenazi synagogues in front of them, in Sephardi ones behind.

The next important part of the synagogue is the platform from which the prayers are conducted and the Torah read. "*Bimah*" is generally the Ashkenazi word for this platform, "*tevah*" the Sephardi. Curiously, Ashkenazi Jews also used the word "*almemar*," from the Arabic "*al-Manbar*," the preacher's pulpit in the mosque. The term "*tevah*" probably originated from the word for the portable chest that once contained the scrolls of the Torah.

The *bimah* apparently emerged from the fusion of two parts of the synagogue that were originally distinct, the *dukhan* or pulpit where the officiating minister stood, in front of the ark, and the table on which the Torah scroll was laid for the reading. This table owes its origin to the platform used during the Temple period for the public reading of the Law on various occasions, including the reading that took place at the end of the Sabbatical year, during the festival of Succoth. In many Ashkenazi synagogues the *dukhan* and the *bimah* remained separate, and the officiating minister used the one or the other for different parts of the service.

In both Ashkenazi and Sephardi synagogues, the *bimah* is in the center of the auditorium, as befits its central function in the services. Its dominant position is conspicuous in illuminations found in medieval *Haggadoth* (the Passover-night liturgy). Next to the ark itself, this elevated platform is the most decorated piece in the synagogue. Railings surround it, except where steps lead up to it. Some illuminations show an entire structure with pillars and roof, reaching up to very near the synagogue ceiling.

Although Maimonides mentions the central positioning of the *bimah* as a religious obligation, we know from synagogues in Provence, Italy, Greece, and Turkey that this was by no means the only location used in the Jewish world. A bipolar structure seems no less legitimate, the ark at the wall facing Jerusalem, the *bimah* at the wall opposite. Steps lead up to the *bimah* from two sides instead of one, and it is higher than the centrally constructed *bimah*. This structure must have had deep roots in Jewish tradition, since it was adopted by Jews in widely distributed communities. In some synagogues in the Balkans and Asia Minor where Sephardi Jews arrived and absorbed the Romaniots, they adopted some Romaniot traditions, including the bipolar structure. In some cases the two systems merged and two *bimah* coexist, each used on specific occasions.

The seating arrangement depended on the location of the *tevah* or *bimah*. In antiquity, few synagogues had fixed seats. Instead, worshipers sat on mats on the floor. Describing the seating in the synagogue, Maimonides says that Jews in the world of Islam sit on mats on the floor, while in Christendom they use benches. He also describes people sitting facing the ark, except the leader of the service, who sits facing the rest of the community. In synagogues dominated by a central *bimah*, particularly among Sephardi and Oriental Jews, people sat all around the synagogue facing the *bimah*. In bipolar synagogues, the benches were on both sides of the *bimah* and the *aron*, facing each other on the right and left, with an empty space or passageway in the middle. Standing on the *bimah*, at the wall opposite the ark, the cantor acted like an orchestra conductor. The entire congregation was visible to him, and remains so in the service today.

In the famous synagogue in Alexandria, people belonging to different crafts sat together. In most synagogues, some seats—the seats near the ark—were considered more prestigious than others; it was the community's leaders who sat closest to Jerusalem. The seat to the ark's right was reserved for the rabbi. In Spanish and Portuguese synagogues in Western Europe and later, from the seventeenth century onward, in the New World, the members of the *Ma'amad* or *Mahamad* (the synagogue's executive board) sat in a "box" in front of the *tevah*.

In many synagogues the seating was the source of a good deal of conflict. Seats could be allocated among members upon the synagogue's inauguration, or they could be sold. Whatever the method of distribution, members soon lost or acquired seats. Through transactions or inheritance, the seats became a commodity that rich people could possess and poor people could often hardly afford. Over time, people inherited seats, so that a man could have a seat in the ladies' gallery and a woman could have one in the men's auditorium.

In ancient times the synagogue was lit with oil lamps. In medieval Europe, though, wax was cheaper, and so candles were used. In Ashkenazi synagogues, two candles burned on either side of the minister's pulpit, or *dukhan*, and an oil lamp burned without interruption before the ark. This lamp, the *Ner-Tamid* (perpetual light), commemorated the eternal light of the Temple. Light was expensive, and Jews donated oil to cover the cost. In some medieval synagogues a special society formed to meet the responsibility of providing oil or wax for the synagogue.

The scrolls of the Torah, placed in the *hekhal* or *aron*, were lovingly adorned. In Oriental and Romaniot synagogues they were kept in an ornamented wooden case that was just a little larger than the scrolls; in Ashkenazi and Italian synagogues they were covered with the finest, most beautifully embroidered cloth mantle the community could afford. In Sephardi synagogues both methods were found. *Rimonim* or *'atarot* (bells and crowns), usually made of silver, embellished the Torah, along with plaques inscribed with the role of that particular scroll, and also with the name of the donor.

Both the decoration and the furnishings of the synagogue reflected the fashion and style of the broader culture. The interior of this building, the Jew's spiritual stronghold, reflected the artistic taste of the Gentile society surrounding it, and other influences from the outside world.[27]

OFFICERS, OFFICIANTS, AND OFFICIALS

The synagogue's social framework is not identical to the social framework of the community; only in small communities with a single synagogue can the leadership of both institutions be the same. In Roman times, the synagogue was administered by the "Head of the Synagogue," the *Rosh Knesset* or *Arcosinagogus*. His position was prestigious and his power extensive, his influence being felt in every field, religious and otherwise. Assisted by a team of officers, he handled the synagogue's administration and upkeep, and usually decided who would officiate in the services. This post gradually lost its power and became an honorary position, sometimes held by women or minors.

In some early medieval communities in various parts of the Jewish world, the head of the synagogue came to be called the "*Parnas*," a title still used today in synagogues of Spanish and Portuguese ancestry in Western Europe and North America. The *Parnas* was expected to be a learned Jew who could lead the congregation in every field relating to the synagogue. The method of his election varied from place to place, from era to era. In a larger congregation he would be assisted by a committee of important *Yehidim* (members), and he also worked closely with the *Gabbay*, the treasurer. In many Ashkenazi and Sephardi synagogues the *Gabbay* was actually the head of the synagogue, suggesting that the collection of money must have been an important administrative function. These leaders belonged to the community's rich elite, a status that changed very little until modern times.

In Roman and Talmudic times there was no synagogue official in charge of conducting the services; the head of the synagogue invited congregants who were versatile in the liturgy and endowed with suitable voices to officiate. The person chosen had to be a worthy Jew, since he acted as the congregation's emissary. When books were handwritten and accordingly rare and expensive, it was imperative that the reader should recite the prayers loudly for the benefit of those who might have erred in their silent prayers.

As knowledge of Hebrew grew meager in many communities, the reading of the Torah became more and more a task for the expert. The first paid official to perform in the service was the *Turgeman*, the translator, appointed in some synagogues in Near Eastern countries early in the Talmudic period. To ensure that the congregation understood the text of the Torah, the *Turgeman* would recite aloud the Aramaic translation of the part of the scroll just read in Hebrew. As the number of people who could read the text of the Torah and chant it according to a special incantation diminished, the reading itself was also eventually handed over to an expert, the *Kore* (reader).

The *Rosh Knesset* of Roman times was assisted by the Hazan, whom the congregation usually respected highly, even though he was a paid official. The Hazan acted under the direct authority of the synagogue leader. His original functions were rather similar to those of the *Shamash* or beadle of post-Talmudic times: he was responsible for the decorum and the smooth running of the services. Acting under the leader's instructions, he would invite the different people who would officiate, preach, or read from Scriptures to perform the parts allocated to them. He would make some of the routine announcements, and in some communities he would act as the *Sofer* or scribe. In later generations, from the sixth century onward, he took the title *Shamash*, but by then the post had begun to lose its previous prestige and its incumbent no longer commanded the congregation's respect, although he remained a powerful figure in the community.[28]

In post-Talmudic times, the title "Hazan" was taken by the officiating minister, who had previously been called the *Shaliah Zibbur* (emissary of the congregation). When the officiating-minister post, a permanent paid position, was created is hard to determine; early allusions to it are not entirely reliable. But it had certainly become necessary by post-Talmudic times, after the sixth century. The minister had to have a grasp of Hebrew, expertise in the reading of the Pentateuchal weekly portion, and vocal and musical excellence. He had to have a knowledge of the prayers, which on festival days were becoming increasingly elaborate and extensive, including passages with which the congregation would not be familiar. These demands joined together to create a post that became central to the synagogue's functioning. There was a time in some regions when a reader recited the prayers while the Hazan performed the musical passages and sang the *piyutim*, the liturgical songs. The two functions eventually became one.

The post of Hazan became essential in the Middle Ages, when most synagogues needed an expert to conduct the services. There were even synagogues in which the women needed a female expert of their own to lead them in their prayers. As the status of the professional reader grew greater in many parts of the Jewish world, the musical traditions too began to assume a new importance. In some ways, in fact, the prayers lost their position to the cantorial performances (though not so far as to erode the requirements for religious and linguistic expertise in the Hazan). Many rabbis were

critical of this development, and would only consider the Hazan's musical talents worthwhile if he used them to instill spiritual inspiration and religious enthusiasm in the congregants. Rabbi Asher ben Yehiel, an eminent rabbi from Germany who settled in Spain at the beginning of the fourteenth century, severely criticized the Spanish Jews because he felt that in appointing their Hazan they were only interested in his voice, and cared little for his religious or moral conduct. There was also strong opposition to cantors who introduced non-Jewish melodies.

With the spread of mechanical printing, the production of prayer books vastly increased. As literacy grew too, the public's dependence on a reader was much reduced. Particularly in Ashkenazi communities, there was a clear decline in the Hazan's status during the transition from the Middle Ages to modern times.

Another of the synagogue's paid officials was the *Darshan*, or preacher. There is evidence that a substantial part of the Midrashic literature was originally transmitted through sermons. The presence of learned discourses in the synagogue does not necessarily imply the appointment of a salaried preacher; some great scholars have been known for their strong and popular sermons, and during Talmudic times (200–500 c.e.), several had the title *Darshan* attached to their name. During the Middle Ages, the character and timing of the sermon changed. The Saturday-morning sermon became less frequent; the Saturday-afternoon sermon became quite an affair. From the sixteenth century on, Sephardi and Ashkenazi preachers followed very different paths. The Sephardi preacher was instrumental in Sephardi communities' quick and successful recovery after the expulsion from Spain. Eastern Europe, on the other hand, became the home of the so-called *Maggid*, the roving preacher who delivered his sermons in Yiddish, which gave them a very popular character. The sermon underwent a radical change in the modern period.

The rabbi, today often considered an integral part of synagogal life, is rather a late development. The scholars of the past were originally independent men, who were not salaried functionaries of the community. The social and economic reasons behind the professionalization of the rabbinate, and the recasting of so many rabbinical scholars as communal functionaries, included persecutions and general insecurity that led to emigration, leaving scholars without a regular income. Most salaried rabbis between the tenth and fourteenth centuries were scholars who had had to abandon their homes; obvious examples are the rabbis from France and Germany who, in the thirteenth and fourteenth centuries, were employed by Spanish communities following expulsions and oppressive measures against the Jews in their own lands. The professionalization of the rabbinate was not a smooth process. It was opposed by various scholars, the most famous of whom was Maimonides.

In the Middle Ages, most scholars and their disciples prayed in the *Beth HaMidrash*, the Talmudic academy. In the modern age, particularly since the last century, the rabbi became the most important official of the synagogue and assumed various tasks there, including that of a regular preacher. In addition to his functions as a teacher, advisor, and sometimes *Dayan* or judge, he participated in the service, reciting some special prayers. Nowadays, most synagogues appoint their own rabbis. In the Reform congregations of nineteenth-century Europe, the rabbi took charge of the services; the post of cantor was canceled in many synagogues. This trend continued in the United States.[29]

THE SYNAGOGUE AS CENTER OF EDUCATION AND LEARNING

Since time immemorial the synagogue has served as a major center of Jewish education for all. The reading from the Torah and the Prophets on Sabbaths, festivals, and special days was designed to educate; both the annual and the triennial cycles of the reading of the Torah were efficient teaching methods. When knowledge of Hebrew declined, it was found necessary to translate the Torah into Aramaic, then widespread among Jews, for simultaneous reading alongside the Hebrew text. Some parts of the service are nothing but the study of the Scriptures and of the Talmudic or Midrashic texts. In antiquity, the sermon and the homiletic exposition of the Scriptures were part of an educational program. In many synagogues, study groups met regularly under the guidance of a scholar. In fact many small synagogues were in reality houses of learning, *Bate Midrash*, more than they were houses of prayer.

The synagogue's educational programs should be examined apart from the elementary education provided for children and from the specialized Talmudic studies in the *Yeshivoth* and *Midrashim*, which were headed by eminent scholars. The synagogue building, however, very often served both systems, so that the atmosphere of learning increased in its precincts.

SOCIAL AND POLITICAL LIFE IN THE SYNAGOGUE

Throughout the ages, the synagogue has been the heart of Jewish community life. For Jews it has been home and castle, the center of their political and social world. The decisions of community leaders and other important announcements would be proclaimed from the *bimah*. Community ordinances or by-laws were usually read out in the synagogue before becoming valid. Some *taqanot* or ordinances stipulated that a certain act or transaction, such as the sale of a property, be read several times in the synagogue before it was implemented. The synagogue was also a political center: local elections might be held

in its annex, and the results announced in the synagogue by the Hazan. The synagogue continued to fulfill these political, administrative, and economic functions as long as the Jews remained relatively autonomous. With the emancipation of the Jews, the synagogue became solely a religious and educational center.

In Western European Ashkenazi synagogues in the twelfth and thirteenth centuries, the custom of "interrupting the prayers" developed as an instrument of pressure on those who failed to comply with a decision of the *Beth Din*, the Jewish court. A man who felt injured by a fellow Jew, and was unable to receive satisfaction from him through litigation, had the right to interrupt the prayers. The service would be suspended until the offender consented to give him satisfaction. As this custom spread, it caused serious disruptions in some synagogues. Several ordinances were passed to end the anarchy it caused: the right to interrupt the prayers might be limited to weekday services, for example, and to the offender's home synagogue rather than the main synagogue of the town.

The sanctity of the synagogue did not prevent people from quarreling and swearing there, and these arguments and curses sometimes led to violence. People who misbehaved in their home and in the street probably didn't change their behavior in the synagogue. In medieval Spain, for instance, violent incidents are recorded of interruptions or disruptions of the services and damage to the furniture. Such reports should not distort the picture of the more usual, ordinary services that ran throughout the year without leaving any record behind.

Most synagogues were controlled by the rich. The poor didn't usually participate much in the services; in some synagogues they had no seats, and were probably uncomfortable during prayers. In some communities confraternities of craftsmen succeeded in establishing their own synagogues. In Zaragoza at the beginning of the fifteenth century, the Bikur Holim (the confraternity for the sick) had its own synagogue. In the same city there was a synagogue for the confraternity of the tanners, and the Sinoga Menor (the smaller synagogue, as opposed to the Sinoga Mayor, the great synagogue) was associated with the Rodfe Zedek, a charitable confraternity. The silversmiths of Zaragoza also had a synagogue of their own. The members of these confraternities must have felt comfortable in their own synagogues, away from the control of the rich. Such synagogues were also found in Eastern Europe.[30]

TRADITION AND MODERNITY

The transformations of the synagogue in the movement from the Middle Ages to modern times were as radical as the transitions that the Jewish people experienced during the same period. No aspect of synagogal life, no part of the synagogue building, was left untouched by change. The innovations were closely related to the emancipation of the Jews of Western Europe: within Jewish society, it was widely agreed that the Jews needed to mend their ways and behave as their Gentile compatriots did. The synagogue did not escape this new spirit.

The first changes were in decorum and discipline. Protagonists of modernity attacked the way Jews behaved in the synagogue, the lack of decorum and aesthetics in the service. Israel Jacobsohn of Kassel was one of the first to introduce changes in his synagogue's services, which he tried to make as similar as possible to those of the Protestant church. He introduced sermons in German, dropped some prayers, and instituted confirmation for boys and girls alike. He also established a choir that sang songs in German. His friend David Friedlander followed a like course in Berlin, suggesting that the "dead" Hebrew language be dropped in favor of German and that all references to Jerusalem or Zion be erased. Friedlander canceled both the *Musaf* or additional service on Sabbaths and festivals and the repetition of the *'Amidah*, the silent prayer. He also adopted the Sephardi pronunciation of Hebrew, probably as a way of breaking with the past.

In 1817, the conflicts caused by these innovations eventually brought the intervention of the Prussian government, which prohibited changes in the traditional form of the service. Friedlander had suggested that he and several other Jews be admitted to the Protestant church, under special conditions; he was refused. Elsewhere, though, changes in the service received support. In France in 1806, Napoleon gathered an "Assembly of Notables" that encouraged reform in the synagogue. The following year, the Great Sanhedrin, the Jews' supreme council, met in Paris and did the same. The Consistoire, the Jewish communal organization created in Napoleonic France, instructed rabbis to preach in the vernacular every Saturday. Jacobsohn exploited the Consistoire's instructions to the full. Some of the changes he introduced were in the fields of decorum and aesthetics; others were more radical, and aroused opposition. When he included Hebrew and German hymns in the new service in the synagogues of Westphalia, for example, many Jews thought he was trying to make the Jewish service look more like the Christian one, and objected strongly. Yet they gradually accepted his innovations—the choir, the stress on decorum and quiet—as necessary ingredients of the service.

The most significant changes were in the structure and contents of the prayers, and the most important reformer here was Wolf Heidenheim, of Berlin. Beginning in 1800, Heidenheim published new editions of the prayer book, with a translation. He omitted all the cabalistic additions, which he considered superfluous and harmful. In Amsterdam in 1795, pro-emancipation elements who had established their own community, Adat Yeshurun, insisted on eliminating any parts of the prayers that contradicted the principles of emancipation.

In 1817, a group of Hamburg Jews founded a society whose aim was to reform Judaism, particularly the services in the "temple." This latter designation was of great ideological significance: asserting the synagogue as the group's temple, it implied that they no longer hoped, prayed for, or even wanted the rebuilding of the Temple in Jerusalem. Indeed their prayer book omitted all messianic passages and references to Jerusalem, the Temple, and sacrifices. The group conducted prayers only on Saturdays and festivals. Other innovations included a choir, the use of an organ, and a sermon in German. They adopted a triennial cycle for the reading of the Torah instead of the annual one in use throughout the world. Taking the Sephardi prayer book as a model, they read many prayers in a new, substantially shorter form. Essentially the Hamburg group carefully expunged all Jewish-nationalistic traits from the prayer book. Theoretically, these changes in the content and form of the prayers were made out of consideration for non-Jewish public opinion.

Traditionalists' opposition to these amendments was vehement and uncompromising. All over Germany, Austria-Hungary, and Italy, rabbis published attacks on them, and prohibited any change in the text of the prayers and the use of musical instruments in the synagogue. The Hamburg Temple failed in leading the immediate revolution that many had expected to win the day. Nevertheless, under its influence or through its inspiration, Reform temples were established in Leipzig, Prague, and Vienna.

In 1841, when the Hamburg Temple published its new prayer book, this conflict within German Jewry was rekindled. The Reform movement now turned to scholars of the caliber of Leopold Zunz and Abraham Geiger, who showed that changes had taken place in the synagogue and its liturgy throughout the ages. The rabbinical reform conferences that were held in 1844, 1845, and 1846 showed how divided opinions were: the language and contents of the prayers were debated but no decision received unanimous support. The prayer book of the Reform community in Berlin underwent a series of revisions in the second part of the nineteenth century, but most Jews did not follow this lead, which they saw as a serious break from tradition. The use of the organ in the service was another subject that was much discussed.

The most serious Reform prayer book, however, published by Abraham Geiger in 1854, eventually came to be used by many congregations. Though the prayers were somewhat shortened, with nationalistic aspirations and wishes for the restoration of sacrifices omitted, they remained in Hebrew. An accompanying text of the prayers in German was a free translation. Reformers continued to propose new prayer books in the years to come.

In many European synagogues, particularly in Italy and France, a choir and sometimes an organ were introduced, and in most liberal synagogues the sermon was delivered in the vernacular. The development of the Reform Movement in England and the United States had serious consequences for contemporary Jewry. In England, the first changes were made by synagogues of the Spanish and Portuguese branch. Throughout Western Europe, these synagogues had already introduced certain changes as a result of their founders' *converso* background: these Jews had been forced to live as Christians before being able to return to Judaism, and even after their return they had retained certain manners and attitudes that had altered the synagogue services. In 1840, English Sephardi and Ashkenazi Jews who were unhappy in their traditional synagogues joined forces to establish a Reform synagogue. Its prayer book omitted the passages relating to sacrifices, but messianic passages remained. The conservative character of the Reform Movement in England led to the emergence of the more radical Liberal and Progressive synagogues.

In the nineteenth century in the United States, Jews still formed a small, loosely organized community. Sermons in English, and an English translation of the traditional prayers, did not prevent some South Carolina Jews from demanding more changes and the use of English in the order of service. When their demands were rejected by the established Jewish community, a group of Jews in Charleston established the Reformed Society of Israelites. Their radical program included shortened prayers, of which a substantial part was in English, and musical instruments accompanying the service. The Protestant influence on these innovations is clear. The Charleston program did not endure, but indicated the trend of the future.

With the arrival of Jewish immigrants from Germany after 1840, Reform synagogues were founded that followed the Hamburg prayer book. An innovation in American Reform synagogues was the adoption of family seating, patterned after the practice in Protestant churches. Reform Judaism reached its most extreme expression in the United States. The Union of American Congregations encompasses synagogues following a variety of practices, but they all share mixed-sex choirs, the use of musical instruments, and the absence of ladies' galleries. *The Union Prayer Book for Jewish Worship*, published in 1894, has become the foundation of the Reform liturgy in America.[31]

Beginning in the 1930s and strengthening after the Holocaust and the creation of the State of Israel, the Reform movement made further changes in certain prayers. Sermons also became less likely to emphasize the universality of the various traits of Judaism and more likely to stress the particularity of the Jewish people's character. At the beginning of the twentieth century, a Conservative Judaism emerged, establishing its own communities and synagogues.[32] Conservative Jews

keep the prayer book almost intact in Hebrew, with some special prayers in English. Certain passages on sacrifices are eliminated. Most synagogues have an organ, and men and women sit together. In recent years a left-wing breakaway group in England, led by Rabbi Louis Jacobs, has established the Mesorati synagogues, similar in concept to the American Conservative synagogues.

Other modern innovations ranged from the special uniform rabbis and cantors came to wear in many synagogues, distinguishing themselves from the rest of the community, to the synagogue's physical structure. In synagogues where men and women sat together, the ladies' galleries or prayer quarters naturally disappeared. Most Orthodox synagogues continued to include a ladies' gallery, but some adopted a more modern approach by allocating part of the auditorium to women, separating it off by a curtain. Another architectural change was the transfer of the *bimah* from the center to the front of the synagogue, next to the ark. Even some Orthodox synagogues have adopted this innovation, for example in the new synagogues in Istanbul. The seating in such synagogues is either in parallel rows facing the ark or in rows arranged in a semicircle, depending on the shape of the auditorium. Another addition inspired by the Christian church was the pulpit for the rabbi's sermon. Synagogues built during the Napoleonic era in areas under French control or influence usually had a pulpit on the left-hand side wall; it was usually made of wood, with stairs leading up to it. In other synagogues the pulpit was either on the *bimah* or to the left of the ark.

The most conspicuous architectural change in modern times is undoubtedly to the synagogue's exterior. With formal emancipation in many European countries and equal rights in the New World, Jews no longer felt the need to pray in a modest building, and began to construct large and impressive synagogues. Care was taken to differentiate the external style from that of the local Christian churches. Thus the great synagogues of Florence and Rome were built in a mixture of Moorish, Assyrian, and Byzantine styles.

Jewish optimism in the period of emancipation, and this desire to make the synagogue architecturally equal to the church, led some communities to initiate projects far beyond their means and needs. Examples may be found in various European lands. In Piemonte, in northwestern Italy, enormous synagogues were built, with gigantic facades, even when the Jewish population was dwindling and the buildings would inevitably be left half empty. Such is the synagogue of Vercelli, today half in ruin. And the city of Turin's most singular monument is a building originally designed as a synagogue, in 1863: the audaciously original and gigantic Mole Antonelliana (named after its architect, Alessandro Antonelli), which reflects the ambitions and exaggerated optimism of the Jews of that time.

EPILOGUE

The synagogue remains to this day the most obvious institution determining Jewish identity. Outside the State of Israel it provides probably the only daily framework within which that identity can be preserved. Place of worship, social center, and school, the synagogue is also the place where Jews, however estranged from tradition, can identify themselves with the Jewish people, Jewish destiny, and Jewish history. If they only attend services two or three times a year, they still feel the need to assert their Jewishness.

Among Ashkenazi Jews in Israel, the division between religious and secular Jews has rigidified: secular Jews no longer feel the need to attend a synagogue in order to feel Jewish. Among Sephardi Jews the polarization remains more moderate, and many Sephardi and Oriental Jews who are not considered religious by generally accepted standards still come to synagogue and take part in the religious life of the community. Whether in Israel or outside it, the synagogue is the institutional stronghold in which Judaism survives as a dynamic, thriving, and constantly developing culture and religion.

NOTES

1. *The Babylonian Talmud*, Seder Nashim, Gittin 56a–b, London: Soncino, 1936, IV:257–58.

2. See Hebrew texts of Jer. 39:8 and Ps. 74:8, respectively.

3. Isa. 56:7.

4. Ezek. 11:16.

5. *The Babylonian Talmud*, Seder Mo'ed, Megillah 29a, IV:175.

6. *The Mishnah*, Yoma, chapter 7, paragraph 1, trans. H. Danby, Oxford, p. 170.

7. *The Mishnah*, Berakhot, chapters 1–5, pp. 2–6.

8. On the development of Jewish liturgy between the first and the eighth centuries, see A. Z. Idelsohn, *Jewish Liturgy and Its Development*, New York, 1931, pp. 26–33.

9. The word, derived from "Rome," refers to the Eastern Roman Empire, that of Byzantium.

10. World War II was disastrous for all the Greek communities, including the four remaining Romaniot communities of Patras, Arta, Ioannina, and Chalkis. In the latter two localities a tiny community has survived until today. In Jerusalem there is a synagogue of Jews originating from Ioannina, which follows some of the Romaniot ritual.

11. See C. Roth, "The Liturgies of Avignon and the Comtat Venaissin," *Journal of Jewish Bibliography* I (1939), and M. Calmann, *The Carrière of Carpentras*, Oxford, 1984, pp. 152–57.

12. For a general survey of all liturgies and the influence of Cabala on the prayerbook, see Idelsohn, pp. 47–70.

13. Deut. 6 and 11, Num. 15.

14. See L. Finkelstein, "The Development of the Amidah," *Jewish Quarterly Review* XVI (1925–26):1f., 127f.; K. Kohler, "The Origin and the Composition of the Eighteen Benedictions," *Hebrew Union College Annual* 1 (1924), pp. 387f.; and M. Liber, "Structure and History of the Tefilah," *Jewish Quarterly Review* XL (1949–50):331f.

15. On the reading from the Pentateuch see J. Mann, *The Bible as Read and Preached in the Old Synagogue*, vol. 1, Cincinnati, 1940, vol. 2, ed. I. Sonne, Cincinnati, 1966. On the triennial cycle, see J. Heinemann, "The Triennial Lectonary Cycle," *Journal of Jewish Studies* XIX (1968):41f.

16. D. de Sola Pool, *The Kaddish*, 2nd ed., New York, 1964.

17. *The Babylonian Talmud*, Seder Zera'im, Berakhot 6a, p. 24.

18. *The Mishnah*, Berakhot, chapter 5, paragraph 1, p. 5.

19. Ps. 16:8.

20. On decorum and behavior in the synagogue, see I. Abrahams, *Jewish Life in the Middle Ages*, New York, 1969, pp. 15–25.

21. Idelsohn, *Jewish Music in Its Historical Development*, New York, 1929.

22. *Tosefta*, Megillah, chapter 4, paragraphs 22–23.

23. See E. W. Goldman, "Samuel Halevi Abulafia's Synagogue (El Tránsito) in Toledo," *Jewish Art* XVIII (1992):59–69.

24. *The Babylonian Talmud*, Seder Zera'im, Berakhot 31a, p. 190.

25. R. Wischnitzer, *The Architecture of the European Synagogue*, Philadelphia, 1964.

26. The Sanctuary, or the Tent of Meeting, was the portable tent in which the Israelite ritual was conducted from the days of Moses until the building of the First Temple by Solomon.

27. On the architecture and interiors of the Spanish synagogues, see Y. Assis, "Synagogues in Medieval Spain," *Jewish Art* XVIII (1992): 14–23; and B. Narkiss, "The Heikhal, Bimah, and the Teivah in Sephardi Synagogues," *Jewish Art* XVIII (1992):31–47.

28. On the *Shamash*, see Abrahams, p. 55ff.

29. I. Levy, *The Synagogue, Its History and Function*, London, 1963, pp. 76–116.

30. On the synagogues of Spanish confraternities, see Assis, pp. 13–14.

31. On the liturgy of Reform Judaism, see Idelsohn, *Jewish Liturgy and Its Development*, pp. 268–300, and J. J. Petuchowski, *Prayerbook Reform in Europe*, New York, 1968.

32. M. Waxman, ed., *Tradition and Change—The Development of Conservative Judaism*, New York, 1958.

ACKNOWLEDGMENTS

Max Richardson deserves my deepest appreciation for the creativity and professionalism he brought to the task of lighting these synagogues under difficult conditions. His assistance and good nature were invaluable.

Anna, my beloved wife, might well have been the subject of the dedication were she not, in fact, the co-author of this book. She not only assisted me in the Caribbean work, she encouraged me from the very beginning and kept our family functioning and in good spirits during my many absences. She is my most useful critic and advisor.

The advice and assistance of the Center for Jewish Art at the Hebrew University of Jerusalem made this project feasible. Seminars in Jewish art, conducted by Professor Bezalel Narkiss and his associates, kindled my enthusiasm for this subject and imparted to me the basic knowledge necessary to pursue it. Professor Narkiss was kind enough to guide me in the selection of synagogues for this book, but the final choices are the responsibility of the editors and myself. Ariella Amar provided valuable information and contacts for the work in Uzbekistan, Poland, and Morocco. Ruti Jacobi's warm encouragement and informative attitude have been much appreciated. Many others at the Center have been helpful in ways too numerous to mention, but Susan Fraiman's initial research and Suzy Sawicki's assistance in the administration of this project have been essential to its success. Here I must say that the intent of this work is neither academic nor strictly documentary. I hope, therefore, that my friends at the Center for Jewish Art will forgive me my shortcomings in these areas and find some pleasure in the beauty and breadth of this work. Rivka and Ben-Zion Dorfman of Jerusalem provided a wealth of information from their personal archives that made the work in Hungary and the Czech Republic possible. Their enthusiasm and willingness to share are an example to me. Orpah Slepak of the Israel Museum in Jerusalem provided contacts and direction that enabled me to work in India.

I am very grateful to Senator Julius Spokojny of the Israelitische Kultursgemeinde Schwaben in Augsburg, who has granted special permission for use of the photos from the Augsburg Synagogue. Many thanks to Mr. Yaakov Margolin of El-Al Israel Airlines for transporting lighting equipment free of charge. El-Al not only got us to and from these locations in safety and comfort, but they did so without delays or loss of baggage. Shmuel Inditski at Hadar Photo Agencies in Tel-Aviv generously loaned Broncolor equipment for the duration of this project. Hadar's excellence in service and facilities is unsurpassed. I am also encouraged by the generous support of the EverColor Corporation of California, which has subsidized a significant portion of the cost of the EverColor pigment-transfer prints for the portfolio and exhibition. The Image Bank offices worldwide provided much practical assistance; in particular, Joachim Soyka's assistance in Munich was essential to the work in Augsburg.

The assistance of individuals and Jewish communities and institutions all over the world have made these photographs possible. I thank all of them for tolerating my intrusions into their synagogues and community life. Many provided hospitality. I cannot list all of them, but there are many individuals who went so far out of their way to assist that I cannot neglect them: Jack and Rudi DeZwart, Zoetermeer, Holland; Nicolle Jally, Paris; Rafi Nektalov, Samarkand and Brooklyn; Albert Weizman, American Joint Distribution Committee, Casablanca; Ya'akov Semana, Casablanca; Ronald and Marilyn Delevante, Kingston, Jamaica; Sarah Pardo, Izmir, Turkey; Professor Nissim Ezekiel, American Joint Distribution Committee, Bombay; Samuel and Len Hallegua, Cochin, India; Bill and Martha Lumm, Port Gibson, Mississippi; Museum of the Southern Jewish Experience, Jackson, Mississippi; and Ewa Wroczyniske, Tykocin, Poland. I am certain that I must have forgotten someone special and trust that their kindness will allow them to forgive me.

The Israel Museum and the Israel Antiquities Authority have extended their permission to reproduce photographs of objects in the Israel Museum.

Jeremy Stavisky and Rabbi Tuvia Kaplan of Jerusalem assisted me in the preparation of the textual material and provided invaluable insights into Jewish law and lore. Zvi Bernstein taught me to learn and love midrashic material. To all of them I am greatly indebted, but only I am responsible for errors of interpretation or translation. The editorial and design staff at Aperture have worked together with me to make this the best book possible; to all of them I am grateful. Finally, I owe Michael Hoffman at Aperture a special debt, for this project was his idea.

A PORTFOLIO
TO COMMEMORATE THE PUBLICATION OF

AND I SHALL DWELL AMONG THEM: HISTORIC SYNAGOGUES OF THE WORLD

TWELVE EVERCOLOR PRINTS
BY NEIL FOLBERG

Szeged, Hungary, page 142; *Ancient Synagogue at Bar Am Israel*, page 146;
Aron Kodesh, Altneushul, Prague, Czech Republic, page 145;
Kehilat Hakodesh, Mad, Hungary, page 126; *Hekhal, Rue Nazareth Synagogue, Paris, France*, page 114;
Spanish-Portuguese Synagogue, Amsterdam, Holland, page 110; *Canton Synagogue, Venice, Italy* page 21;
Rubinov House Synagogue, Bukhara, Uzbekistan, page 54; *Suiri Synagogue, Tangiers, Morocco*, page 34;
Porch, Beit-El Synagogue, Raudenda, India, page 69;
Temple Gemiluth Chessed, Port Gibson, Mississippi, U.S. page 82; *Ades Synagogue, Jerusalem, Israel*, page 151.

THE EDITION IS LIMITED TO FIFTY NUMBERED AND TEN LETTERED PORTFOLIOS.
EACH PRINT IS SIGNED BY THE ARTIST AND EDITIONED. THE IMAGE SIZE IS 11 X 14 INCHES.

THE PORTFOLIO IS AVAILABLE FROM
APERTURE, 20 EAST 23RD STREET, NEW YORK, NEW YORK 10010
TELEPHONE (212) 598-4205. FAX (212) 598-4015

Library of Congress Catalog Card Number: 95-76134

Hardcover ISBN: 0-89381-640-X

Book design by Wendy Byrne

Color separation by Sele Offset Turin, Paris, New York
Printed and bound by Mariogros Industrie Grafiche,
Turin, Italy

The Staff at Aperture for *And I Shall Dwell Among Them:
Historic Synagogues of the World* is:
Michael E. Hoffman, *Executive Director;*
Michael Sand, *Editor;* Diana C. Stoll, *Associate Editor;*
Stevan A. Baron, *Production Director;* Sandra Greve,
Production Manager; Michael Lorenzini, *Editorial Assistant;*
Lara Frankena, *Editorial Work-Scholar;* Laurie Burgan,
Production Work-Scholar

Aperture Foundation publishes a periodical, books, and
portfolios of fine photography to communicate with
serious photographers and creative people everywhere.
A complete catalog is available upon request.
Address: 20 East 23rd Street, New York, NY 10010.
Phone: (212) 598-4205. Fax: (212) 598-4015.

First edition   10 9 8 7 6 5 4 3 2 1